PINK EDITION

DAILY NEWS

New York's Picture Newspaper

2¢

Vol. 26. No. 267

New York, Wednesday, May 2, 1945

NAZI RADIO ANNOUNCES:

HITLER DEAD

'FELL IN COMMAND POST'

ADM. DOENITZ NAMED HEAD OF REICH, ARMY

Story on Page 3

HITLER'S
LAST DAYS

HITLER'S
LAST DAYS

THE DEATH OF THE NAZI REGIME AND
THE WORLD'S MOST NOTORIOUS DICTATOR

BILL O'REILLY

SQUARE
FISH

Henry Holt and Company

NEW YORK

SQUARE
FISH

An imprint of Macmillan Publishing Group, LLC
175 Fifth Avenue
New York, NY 10010
fiercereads.com

Square Fish and the Square Fish logo are trademarks of Macmillan and are used by
Henry Holt and Company under license from Macmillan.

Our books may be purchased in bulk for promotional, educational, or business use. Please contact your
local bookseller or the Macmillan Corporate and Premium Sales Department at (800) 221-7945
ext. 5442 or by e-mail at MacmillanSpecialMarkets@macmillan.com.

Permission to use the following images is gratefully acknowledged (additional credits are noted with captions):
Mary Evans Picture Library—endpapers, pp. ii, v, vi, 35, 135, 248, 251; Bridgeman Art Library—endpapers,
p. iii; Heinrich Hoffman/Getty—p. 1. All maps by Gene Thorp.

Library of Congress Cataloging-in-Publication Data
O'Reilly, Bill.
Hitler's last days : the death of the Nazi regime and the world's
most notorious dictator / Bill O'Reilly. —
pages   cm
Includes bibliographical references and index.
ISBN 978-1-250-08859-8 (paperback)   ISBN 978-1-62779-397-1 (ebook)
1. Hitler, Adolf, 1889–1945.   2. Hitler, Adolf, 1889–1945—Death and burial.
3. World War, 1939–1945—Campaigns—Germany.   4. Berlin, Battle of, Berlin, Germany,
1945.   5. Heads of state—Germany—Biography.   6. Dictators—Germany—
Biography.   I. O'Reilly, Bill. Killing Patton. II. Title.
DD247.H5O735 2015   943.086092—dc23   2015000562

Based on the book *Killing Patton* by Bill O'Reilly, originally published in
the United States by Henry Holt and Company
First Square Fish Edition: 2017
Book designed by Meredith Pratt
Square Fish logo designed by Filomena Tuosto

1   3   5   7   9   10   8   6   4   2

AR: 8.1 / LEXILE: 1160L

I do not see why man should not be
just as cruel as nature.
—ADOLF HITLER

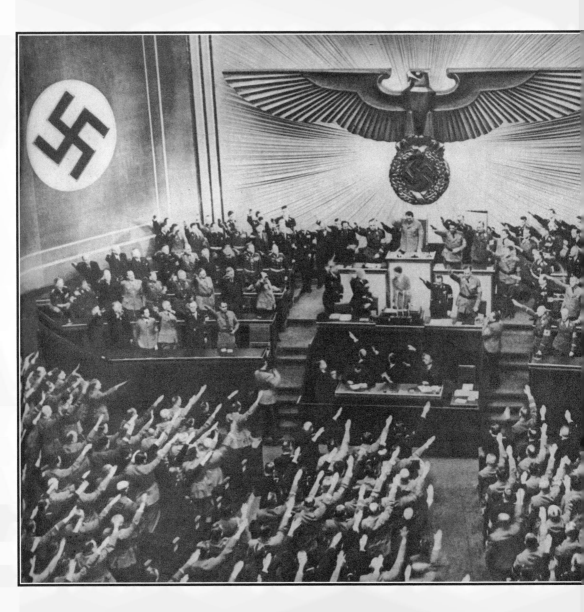

CONTENTS

Map Legend

Allied

➡ Advance

⇨ Highlighted movement

┄┄➤ Retreat

🧍 Infantry

 Armor/ mechanized*
U.S./U.K.

U.S.S.R.

Axis

⬅ Advance

⇦ Highlighted movement

┄┄➤ Retreat

🧍 Infantry

 Armor/ mechanized*

*On some maps, only tank symbols are used. In these cases, tanks represent armies or army groups that also include infantry.

White symbols are used periodically to highlight Allied units and their movements.

Military features

〰 Front line

〰 Defensive position

〰 West Wall

✶ Clash/event

Battery

Machine-gun emplacement

▨ Barbwire

Physical features

〜 Major roads

〜 Minor roads

〜 Railroads

〜 Rivers

Terrain

Forest

○ City/town with urban area

Combatant nationalities

🇺🇸 United States

🇬🇧 United Kingdom

Canada

🇫🇷 France

U.S.S.R.

Germany

A NOTE TO READERS

I THINK IT FAIR TO SAY that people who make history are some of the boldest people to have ever walked the earth. Researching and writing about them can be sobering, time consuming, and full of discovery.

Working on this book was a journey. It began in the German town of Heidelberg, with a visit to the hospital room at Nachrichten Kaserne where General George S. Patton died. It also included many conversations with the personal staff and others close to Adolf Hitler. Some of this was a straightforward dig into various archives, museums, and official U.S. Army battlefield histories. But it didn't just involve reading published works. It involved speaking and corresponding with descendants of those who were actually there like Hitler's secretary. Hitler's former clerks verified his last days with vivid portrayals in German. I talked with the grandchildren and learned about his crazy hour-by-hour situation and the extreme measures he took to stay alert, like cocaine eyedrops. The search for information led to local historians, to Luxembourg, and to Germany—nothing was left unexplored.

Adolf Hitler is modern history's best-known evil ruler and murderer, so to step inside his world is frightening, to say the least. From his early days as chancellor of Germany to his last days as Führer before his suicide, Hitler's life—and death—were filled with senseless violence. But this is not just a story about the world's most notorious dictator. It's a story about the last six months of World War II, and the chaos and brutality that characterized this period of history. It is a story about the people who fought—the flesh-and-blood men and women who laid down their lives in this great tragedy. And it's about the military leaders who strategized and maneuvered to bring the war to a close. In this book, they aren't just famous people to study; they are human beings.

Hitler's Last Days is ultimately a story about a struggle for power. And with that, I put you right in the bunker.

Bill O'Reilly
New York

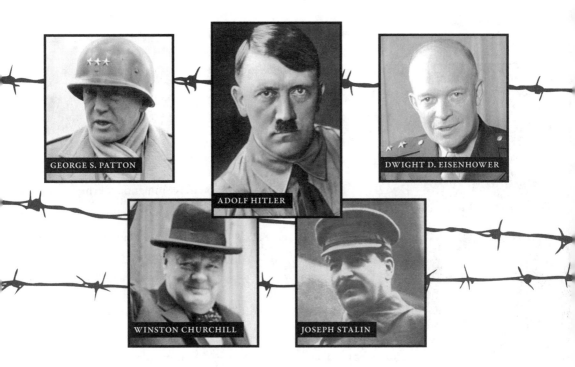

GEORGE S. PATTON

ADOLF HITLER

DWIGHT D. EISENHOWER

WINSTON CHURCHILL

JOSEPH STALIN

KEY PLAYERS

UNITED STATES

Creighton Abrams: Lieutenant colonel, commander of U.S. Thirty-Seventh Tank Battalion, Fourth Armored Division

Charles Boggess: First lieutenant, U.S. Thirty-Seventh Tank Battalion

Omar Bradley: Lieutenant general, commander of U.S. Twelfth Army Group, which includes Third Army

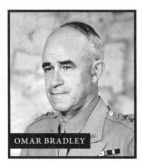

OMAR BRADLEY

OSCAR KOCH

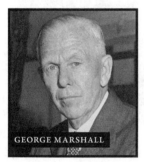

GEORGE MARSHALL

Charles Codman: Colonel, General Patton's aide-de-camp

Jacob Devers: Lieutenant general, commander of the U.S. Sixth Army Group

Benjamin Dickson: Colonel, U.S. First Army intelligence chief (G-2)

Dwight D. Eisenhower: General, supreme commander of the Allied Expeditionary Force in Europe

Hugh Gaffey: Major general, commander of U.S. Fourth Armored Division, Third Army

Paul Harkins: Colonel, General Patton's deputy chief of staff

Joseph Harper: Colonel, commander of U.S. 327th Glider Infantry Regiment

Courtney Hodges: Lieutenant general, commander of U.S. First Army

Harry Kinnard: Lieutenant colonel, U.S. 101st Airborne Division operations officer

Oscar Koch: Colonel, U.S. Third Army intelligence chief (G-2)

George Marshall: General, chief of staff of the U.S. Army

Anthony McAuliffe: Brigadier general, acting commander of U.S. 101st Airborne Division

Troy Middleton: Lieutenant general, commander of U.S. Eighth Corps, Third Army

ANTHONY McAULIFFE

John Mims: Sergeant, General Patton's driver

Ned Moore: Lieutenant colonel, General McAuliffe's chief of staff

Beatrice Patton: George Patton's wife

George S. Patton: General, commander of U.S. Third Army

Franklin Delano Roosevelt: President of the United States of America

JOSEPH STALIN AND
FRANKLIN DELANO ROOSEVELT

BRITAIN

Winston Churchill: Prime minister of the United Kingdom of Great Britain and Northern Ireland

Bernard Montgomery: British field marshal, commander of Twenty-First Army Group, which included British and Canadian forces

Kenneth Strong: British major general, General Eisenhower's intelligence chief (G-2)

RUSSIA

Joseph Stalin: Premier of the Soviet Union

BERNARD MONTGOMERY

MARTIN BORMANN

HEINRICH HIMMLER

WILHELM KEITEL

GERMANY

Martin Bormann: Head of Nazi Party Chancellery

Eva Braun: Hitler's mistress, then wife

Joseph Goebbels: Reich minister of propaganda

EVA BRAUN

Heinrich Himmler: Reichsführer of the SS

Adolf Hitler: Führer of Germany and leader of the Nazi Party

Traudl Junge: one of Hitler's secretaries

Wilhelm Keitel: Field marshal, Hitler's commander of the armed forces

Heinrich Lüttwitz: General, commander of German panzer troops surrounding Bastogne

Theodor Morell: Hitler's personal doctor

Joachim Peiper: German SS commander, First SS Panzer Division

Erwin Rommel: German field marshal

Christa Schroeder: one of Hitler's secretaries

Otto Skorzeny: German SS officer

Albert Speer: Hitler's minister of armaments

Gerd von Rundstedt: German field marshal, western front

Walther Wenck: General, German Twelfth Army

ERWIN ROMMEL

PART ONE

THE WOLF'S LAIR

CHAPTER 1

THE WOLF'S LAIR

EAST PRUSSIA ✠ OCTOBER 21, 1944 ✠ 9:30 A.M.

I N 190 DAYS THE WOLF will be dead.

Today he limps through the woods. The autumn air is chill and damp. As he does each morning at just about this time, Adolf Hitler, Führer of Germany and leader of the Nazi Party, emerges from the artificial light of his concrete bunker into the morning sun. He holds his German shepherd, Blondi, on a short leash for their daily walk through the thick birch forest. A fussy man of modest height and weight who is prone to emotional outbursts, Hitler wears his dark brown hair parted on the right and keeps his mustache carefully combed and trimmed. When Hitler was a young soldier, he preferred a long mustache and would curl the ends, but in World War I that style interfered with the seal on the

Adolf Hitler, early 1944. [Mary Evans Picture Library]

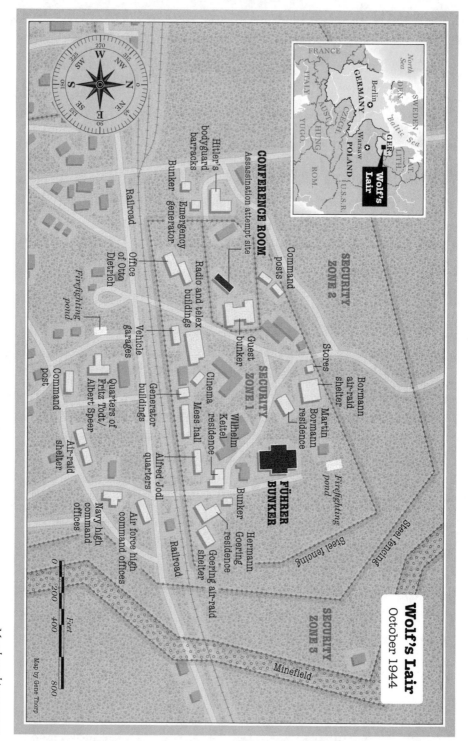

Wolf's Lair
October 1944

FRANCE — North Sea — SWEDEN — DEN. — Baltic Sea — GERMANY — Berlin — POLAND — Warsaw — GER. — Wolf's Lair — LITH. — LAT. — U.S.S.R. — CZECH. — AUST. — HUNG. — ROM. — YUGO. — ITALY

CONFERENCE ROOM
Assassination attempt site

Hitler's bodyguard barracks

Bunker

Emergency generator

Office of Otto Dietrich

Radio and telex buildings

Firefighting pond

Vehicle garages

Command posts

Guest bunker

SECURITY ZONE 1

SECURITY ZONE 2

Stores

Bormann air-raid shelter

Martin Bormann residence

Firefighting pond

Cinema

Wilhelm Keitel residence

Mess hall

Generator buildings

Quarters of Fritz Todt/ Albert Speer

Command post

Air-raid shelter

Alfred Jodl quarters

Navy high command offices

Air force high command offices

Railroad

Railroad

FÜHRER BUNKER

Hermann Goering residence

Goering air-raid shelter

Steel fencing

Steel fencing

SECURITY ZONE 3

Minefield

0 200 400 800

Feet

Map by Gene Thorp

Map legend is on page x.

gas mask he was required to wear. He cut off the ends, leaving only the center patch—called a toothbrush mustache.

Hitler spends more time at the Wolf's Lair, his extensive headquarters in the far eastern outpost of Germany called East Prussia, than in Berlin—some eight hundred days in the last three years. The Führer is fond of saying that his military planners chose the "most marshy, mosquito-ridden, and climatically unpleasant place possible" for this hidden headquarters when they scouted its location in 1940—a fact that is quite real on humid summer days.

The air is so heavy and thick with clouds of mosquitoes that Hitler prefers to remain in the cool confines of his bunker all day long.

But autumn is different. The forests of East Prussia have a charm all their own this time of year, and Hitler needs no convincing to venture outside for his daily walk. These long morning strolls are a vital part of the Führer's day, offering him a

Hitler plays with his German shepherd, Blondi, at one of his mountain homes.
[Mary Evans Picture Library]

chance to compose his thoughts before long afternoons of war strategizing and policy meetings. Sometimes he amuses himself by teaching Blondi tricks, such as climbing a ladder or balancing on a narrow pole.

The journey through the dictator's six hundred-acre wooded hideaway takes Hitler and Blondi past concrete bunkers, personal residences, soldiers' barracks, a power plant, and even the demolished conference room where just three months ago Hitler was almost killed by an assassin's bomb. But despite all these visible reminders that the Wolf's Lair is a military headquarters, and despite the fact that his country is on the verge of losing the greatest war the world has ever known, the fifty-five-year-old Nazi dictator, who likes the nickname Wolf, strolls with an outward air of contentment, utterly lost in thought.

But Hitler is not tranquil. His right eardrum was ruptured by the blast of the assassin's bomb and has only recently stopped bleeding. That same blast hurled him to a concrete floor, bruising his buttocks "as blue as a baboon's behind"

Hitler examines the damage done in the plot to assassinate him. The man on the left is Benito Mussolini, Italy's prime minister and Hitler's strongest ally. [Mary Evans Picture Library]

and filling his legs with wooden splinters as it ripped his black uniform pants to shreds.

However, the failed assassination plot, engineered by members of the German military, did not cause all of Hitler's health issues. His hands and left leg have long trembled from anxiety. He is prone to dizziness, high blood pressure, and stomach cramps. The skin beneath his uniform is the whitest white because he does not spend time in the sun. And his energy is often so low that Theodor Morell, his longtime personal doctor, makes it a practice to inject Hitler each day with the stimulant methamphetamine. The doctor also places drops containing cocaine in each of the Führer's dark blue eyes in order to give the dictator a daily rush of euphoria.

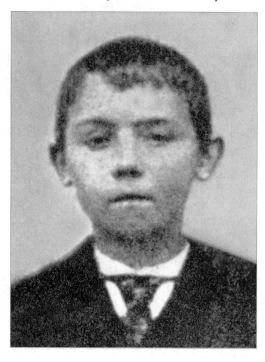

Adolf Hitler does not seem to have been a sickly child, although the reality and the myths of that childhood are vastly different. While he told people that he had struggled up from poverty, in fact he was born into a middle-class household and never expected that he would have to work for a living

Hitler in 1899, about age ten. [Mary Evans Picture Library]

but would live on his family's savings. While he had dreams of being a famous architectural artist, he had not done well enough in school to get into the Academy of Fine Arts in Vienna. This man, who would later command thousands with horrible charisma, was shy and usually silent as a child.

And so the reality and the myths of the current situation reflect this lifelong dichotomy. Despite recent German setbacks on the battlefield, the Wolf still has hope that his plans for global domination will be realized. His greatest goal is the eradication of the Jewish people, with whom he is obsessed. "This war can end two ways," he said in January 1942, addressing a mass rally at the Berlin Sportpalast. "Either the extermination of the Aryan [term used by the Nazis to mean non-Jewish Caucasians with Nordic features] people or the disappearance of Jewry from Europe."

Hitler fancies himself a military strategist, despite no formal training in field tactics. He takes full credit for the great U.S. General George S. Patton's recent defeat at Fort Driant in occupied France, in a long close-range battle that caused Patton to retreat south to the town of Nancy to regroup his vast Third Army. Hitler is cheered by the news that Nazi scientists are very close to developing a bomb with nuclear capacity, a weapon that would allow him to wipe his enemies off the face of the earth. In addition, he is quite sure that the audacious surprise attack he will unveil to his top commanders in a few short hours will push the Allied armies back across France and will allow Germany to regain control of Europe.

And most of all, Adolf Hitler is finally rid of those top

generals who have long despised him. SS death squads hunted down each of the men who took part in the July 20 assassination plot. Some were shot immediately, which infuriated Hitler because such a death was far too quick. So on his orders, the others were hanged. A cameraman filmed the events for Hitler's enjoyment.

Among those accused of treason was Hitler's favorite general, Field Marshal Erwin Rommel. Just seven days ago, his house was surrounded by SS soldiers. Although he did not take an active part, Rommel knew of the plot to assassinate Hitler but did not warn him. This made him as guilty as the man who concealed the bomb in a briefcase and carried it into Hitler's conference room. Rommel kept silent because he had grave doubts about Hitler's ability to lead the war effort and favored suing for peace with the Allies rather than continuing a conflict that was destroying all of Germany. Because of his extraordinary service to the Third Reich, Rommel was given discretionary treatment. He was offered the option of swallowing a cyanide pill rather than going through a public trial.

The SS troopers drove Rommel away from his home, stopped in a quiet forest, surrounded the car, and handed him the pill. Fifteen minutes later, the general whom the Allied leaders—Supreme Allied Commander Dwight D. Eisenhower, British Field Marshal Bernard Montgomery, U.S. General George Patton, and U.S.

German Field Marshal Erwin Rommel in 1942. [Mary Evans Picture Library]

General Omar Bradley—respected for his intelligence and military trade craft and considered their true opponent is dead.

The Wolf could have waited until after his new offensive plan was completed to pass judgment on his favorite field marshal. From a tactical perspective, it would have been the smart thing to do. But Adolf Hitler needed his revenge. Nothing—not even winning the war—mattered more.

Hitler and Blondi finish their walk and reenter the massive concrete fortress that serves as his home away from Berlin. It is almost time for lunch—and the unveiling of his brilliant new campaign.

Or, as it will soon become known around the world: the Battle of the Bulge.

CHAPTER 2

GENERAL PATTON'S HEADQUARTERS

NANCY, FRANCE ✠ OCTOBER 21, 1944

GEORGE S. PATTON THINKS SO HIGHLY of Field Marshal Erwin Rommel that he keeps a copy of Rommel's book on infantry tactics near his bedside. Often, when he is unable to sleep, Patton opens it to reread a chapter or two. But while the two great generals did not collide in the North African desert, the contest between Rommel, the Desert Fox, and another Allied commander, British Field Marshal Bernard Montgomery, ended in Tunisia in May 1943 with the Axis troops surrounded.

Patton's Third Army did not become active on the European front until two months after D-day, June 6, 1944. He then directed the successful U.S. Third Army march across France and is now in position near the southern border between France and Germany. Patton considers the effort stalled because General Dwight D. Eisenhower has ordered him to stop his army

Troops at rest check their vehicles on the march across Belgium, early November 1944.
[Library of Congress]

and regroup. And so begins the October pause. The lull in the action is a foolish move on Eisenhower's part. The American army might be using the lull to reinforce, but so are the Germans. Unbeknownst to the Americans, Adolf Hitler is planning a major attack of his own.

General George S. Patton in 1944. [Mary Evans Picture Library]

CHAPTER 3

THE WOLF'S LAIR

EAST PRUSSIA ✠ OCTOBER 21, 1944

HITLER IS MEETING IN PRIVATE with one of his devoted followers, SS officer Otto Skorzeny. At six feet four, the legendary commando stands a half foot taller than the Führer. If Erwin Rommel was once Hitler's favorite general, then the Long Jumper, as Skorzeny is nicknamed, is Hitler's favorite commando. Time and again, the gruff Austrian has shown his loyalty to the Führer by accepting missions that other men would refuse on the grounds that they were impossible or suicidal.

The Führer turns to Skorzeny and says, "In December, Germany will start a great offensive which may well decide her fate. The world thinks Germany is finished, with only the day

SS officer Otto Skorzeny in 1943. [Mary Evans Picture Library]

and the hour of the funeral to be named. I am going to show them how wrong they are. The corpse will rise and throw itself at the West."

The Führer has done away with those who might be disloyal to him, and he is building his battle plans around loyal worshippers like Otto Skorzeny. So even though Erwin Rommel, with his unmatched prowess as a commander of panzer troops, is gone forever, Hitler is confident of success. He is also well aware that his tank commanders will not have to face George S. Patton and his Third Army, because the secret offensive is deliberately being launched in a battlefield too far north for Patton and his brilliant tactical mind to reach in time.

Hitler then tells his favorite commando and fellow Austrian the details of the coming offensive. He is sure that Skorzeny and his men are more than capable of playing a pivotal role in this surprise attack, known as Operation Watch on the Rhine, but that is not how Hitler intends to use them.

Hitler directs Skorzeny and his men to infiltrate enemy lines by dressing in American uniforms and pretending to be U.S. soldiers. They will all speak English and will sow confusion by spreading false rumors, capturing vital bridges, and killing Americans caught by surprise. The most important rumor is one meant to cause fear and distraction in the highest levels of Allied leadership: that Skorzeny is en route to Paris to kidnap General Dwight D. Eisenhower.

"I am giving you unlimited power to set up your brigade. Use it, colonel!" Hitler says triumphantly.

Skorzeny breaks into a broad smile as he realizes that he has just risen in rank.

CHAPTER 4

TRIANON PALACE HOTEL

VERSAILLES, FRANCE ✠ OCTOBER 21, 1944 ✠ EARLY AFTERNOON

A T THE EXACT MOMENT THAT Hitler is briefing Skorzeny, General Dwight Eisenhower lights a cigarette in his first-floor office. His headquarters, a white stone French château one thousand miles west of the Wolf's Lair, is spotless and regal. The only challenge Eisenhower should be facing right now is how best to celebrate a major turning point in the war. The American army has spent weeks leveling the German city of Aachen. Any moment now, Eisenhower should be receiving word that the city has become the first German municipality to fall into Allied hands. There is widespread hope that this marks the beginning of the end for the Nazi war machine and that the fighting will end by New Year's Eve.

Eisenhower smokes and paces. The fifty-four-year-old general played football back in his days at the U.S. Military Academy at

General Dwight David "Ike" Eisenhower, in an official portrait.
[Mary Evans Picture Library]

West Point, but now he carries a small paunch and walks with his shoulders rolled forward. For security purposes, there is not a situation map tacked to the plywood partition in his office. Instead, he carries details of the German, British, and American armies in his head.

Eisenhower is plagued by a daily list of worries. If anything, his life since becoming supreme commander of the Allied force in Europe has been one headache after another, punctuated by moments of world-changing success. But these new expectations about the war's end worry Ike deeply right now. He is well aware that the proposed New Year's date to end the war will be impossible. Yet his boss, army Chief of Staff George Marshall, has set this date in stone. Hence the deep frown lines on Eisenhower's

American infantrymen on their way to Belgium. [Mary Evans Picture Library]

high, bald forehead. Marshall is back in Washington, thirty-nine hundred miles from the front. He is chief of staff of the army and chief military adviser to President Roosevelt. No other officer in the combined Allied armies has more power and influence than he does.

Marshall just returned to the United States after a weeklong tour of the European theater of operations, whereupon he cabled Eisenhower his great displeasure about the strategic situation. The October pause brought on by poor logistics, which so enrages George Patton, infuriates Marshall, too. He is demanding an end to the stalemate. Everything possible must be done to attack deep into Germany and end the war by the new year.

Per Marshall's orders, this is to include using weapons currently considered top secret and placing every single available American, British, and Canadian soldier on the front lines. Nothing must be held back.

Eisenhower must find a way. Orders are orders. And his success has been largely based on obeying them. So Ike paces and smokes. A few top American generals are coming over for dinner tonight. The celebration of Aachen can wait until then.

So Eisenhower is faced with the stark reality that the lack of gas, guns, and bullets afflicts all the Allied forces up and down the five hundred miles of front lines. They are, for the most part, stuck and immobile. Eisenhower knows that Adolf Hitler and the armies of Nazi Germany are far from conquered.

◆　◆　◆

What Eisenhower doesn't know is that German soldiers, guns, and tanks are quietly grouping near the German border. They do so under strict radio silence, lest the Americans hear their chatter and anticipate the biggest surprise attack since Pearl Harbor.

The Germans face west, toward the American lines and the thick wilderness of a place in Belgium known as the Ardennes Forest. It is here that U.S. forces are weakest because it is assumed that an attack through this dense wood is impossible. To tilt the odds even further in the Germans' favor, they know that George Patton and his Third Army are more than one hundred miles southeast, still in dire need of gas, guns, and soldiers.

So Operation Watch on the Rhine will be a successful counterattack that not even the great George Patton can thwart—of that Hitler and his generals are sure.

The Nazis are poised to turn defeat into victory with this counterattack and the development of a new atomic weapon that Hitler believes is almost ready.

The Führer is still certain of ultimate victory.

Very certain.

CHAPTER 5

WAR ROOM, U.S. THIRD ARMY HEADQUARTERS

NANCY, FRANCE ✠ DECEMBER 9, 1944 ✠ 7 A.M.

COLONEL OSCAR KOCH THINKS THAT Hitler is up to something.

The G-2, as General George Patton's top intelligence officer is known in military vocabulary, is also certain that the German army is far from defeated. In fact, he is the only intelligence officer on the Allied side who is quite sure that Germany is poised to launch a withering Christmas counterattack.

Only nobody will listen to him.

The sun has not yet risen on what promises to be another bitter cold and wet day in eastern France. Koch stands amidst the countless maps lining the walls of the war room, sixty miles south of the front lines. The forty-seven-year-old career soldier is bald and stands ramrod straight, with thick glasses that give him a professorial air.

Just a few feet away, George S. Patton sits in a straight-backed wooden chair as Koch begins the morning intelligence briefing. Patton wears a long overcoat and scarf to ward off the cold, even indoors. He is pensive, and eager to once again be on the attack. In just ten short days, Patton is launching Operation Tink, which will take his Third Army into Nazi Germany for the first time. The invasion of Germany now awaits. Patton plans to cross the Rhine and press hard toward Frankfurt, then on to Berlin.

Colonel Oscar Koch. [U.S. Army Archive]

Unlike many generals, who plan an attack without first consulting with their G-2, Patton relies heavily on Koch.

And with good reason. A humble veteran soldier who made his way up through the ranks, Koch is perhaps the hardest-working man on Patton's staff. He is consumed with the task of collecting information about every aspect of the battlefield. Koch arranges for reconnaissance planes to fly over enemy positions, and then has a team of draftsmen construct precise terrain maps of the

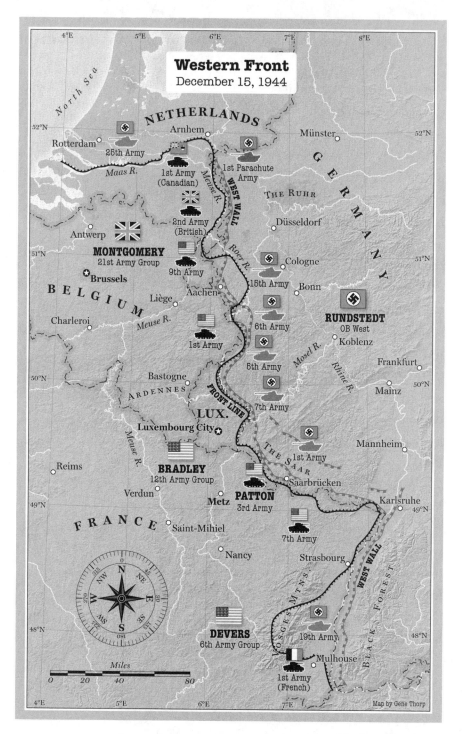

Western Front
December 15, 1944

North Sea

4°E 5°E 6°E 7°E 8°E

NETHERLANDS

52°N Arnhem Münster 52°N

Rotterdam

25th Army

Maas R.

1st Army
(Canadian)

1st Parachute
Army

Meuse R.

WEST WALL

THE RUHR

GERMANY

2nd Army
(British)

Düsseldorf

Antwerp

51°N Roer R. Cologne 51°N

MONTGOMERY
21st Army Group

9th Army

15th Army Bonn

Brussels

BELGIUM Liège Aachen

Charleroi

Meuse R.

6th Army

RUNDSTEDT
OB West

Koblenz

1st Army

5th Army

Mosel R.

Rhine R.

Frankfurt

50°N Bastogne 50°N

ARDENNES

FRONT LINE

7th Army

Mainz

LUX.

Luxembourg City

THE SAAR

1st Army

Mannheim

Reims

Meuse R.

BRADLEY
12th Army Group

Saarbrücken

Verdun Metz

PATTON
3rd Army

Karlsruhe

49°N Saint-Mihiel 49°N

FRANCE

7th Army

N

NW NE

W E

SW SE

S

Nancy

Strasbourg

VOSGES MTNS.

WEST WALL

BLACK FOREST

DEVERS
6th Army Group

48°N 19th Army 48°N

Miles

0 20 40 80

1st Army
(French)

Mulhouse

4°E 5°E 6°E 7°E

Map by Gene Thorp

Map legend is on page x.

towns, rivers, railway lines, fence lines, creeks, farm buildings, bridges, and other obstacles that might slow down the Third Army's advance.

Koch also arranges for German-speaking American soldiers to exchange their military uniforms for peasant clothing at night, then travel behind enemy lines and mingle in bars and restaurants to collect information about German troop movements.

And Koch sees to it that data radioed back from the front lines by American patrols is carefully scrutinized.

Every bit of that information comes together in the war room's centerpiece, an enormous series of maps detailing the entire western front. British, American, Canadian, French, and German positions are all carefully pinpointed.

The maps' transparent acetate coverings are marked in grease pencil, with special notations for armored, infantry, and artillery. Each unit has a unique symbol. Once an army is on the move, its progress is closely tracked. A wet rag wipes the acetate clean, and a unit's new location is at once marked in grease pencil. In this way, Colonel Oscar Koch knows with almost pinpoint accuracy the location of every tank, artillery, airfield, fuel dump, supply depot, railway station, and infantry detachment between Antwerp and Switzerland.

And that, Koch now explains to Patton as the general listens with his usual intensity, is what troubles him. There is something missing.

The Third Army's proposed route across the Rhine and into

Germany is defended by a small and vulnerable German force. So, in all likelihood, Patton's Operation Tink will begin as a rousing success—though Koch never goes out on a limb to predict a victory. War is too uncertain.

But Koch goes on to point out that a real problem lies farther north, on what will be Third Army's left flank during Operation Tink.

In particular, Koch is worried about an enormous German troop buildup. Although the roads are empty during daylight hours, Koch has discovered that thirteen enemy infantry divisions have been relocated under the cover of darkness to an area near the Ardennes Forest. This means an additional two hundred thousand German soldiers at the precise location where the U.S. lines are at their thinnest. German forces in the Ardennes currently outnumber Americans by more than two to one.

In addition, advance scouts from U.S. General Courtney Hodges's First Army report that they clearly hear the rumble of truck engines and the heavy clank of tank treads coming through the forest from the German lines. Koch has confirmed that five panzer divisions containing some five hundred tanks recently moved toward the Ardennes. Also, German railway cars loaded with men and ammunition are proceeding toward the Ardennes with increasing frequency. Just three days ago, a coded message intercepted by the Allies showed that a major German fighting force had requested fighter plane protection as they moved troops and supplies toward the Ardennes.

Perhaps spookiest of all: The Germans have shrouded this major movement in complete radio silence.

Koch does not have to remind Patton that radio silence usually precedes an attack.

Patton quietly absorbs what Koch has to say, sometimes taking notes or interrupting with a specific question. Despite believing that Koch is "the best damned intelligence officer in any United States command," the general is well aware that every single other Allied intelligence analyst believes the Germans are too beaten down to launch a major offensive.

Should it take place, a German attack would be launched against positions currently occupied by the U.S. First Army. But the First's G-2, Colonel Benjamin "Monk" Dickson, is not concerned. He does not believe that the Germans pose a threat. Though he knows about the hundreds of panzers, the railway cars packed with elite SS divisions, and the sudden appearance of German fighter planes in the sky after months of Allied air superiority, Dickson prefers to believe that the German movement is a regular rotation of troops in and out of the area.

This lack of concern is mirrored throughout the highest levels of the Allied command. British Field Marshal Bernard Montgomery writes to a fellow British general that Hitler "is fighting a defensive campaign on all fronts. He cannot stage a major offensive operation." Monty is so certain there will not be a surprise attack that he is making plans to return home to London for Christmas.

Colonel Oscar Koch is the only man who believes that the Germans are ready to attack. He ends his briefing. Patton's excitement about Operation Tink is temporarily set aside as he absorbs the heavy weight of this new information. The general knows that Koch is a cautious man and reluctant to speculate, preferring to speak in hard facts. So for the G-2 to insist that a major new German attack is almost certain means a great deal.

Patton does not rise to his feet for quite some time. He silently ponders another situation that has been nagging at him: Despite aggressive Third Army patrols into Germany's Saar region in the past few weeks, there has been almost no enemy resistance. This is very unusual. The Germans normally fight viciously for every inch of ground. Patton finds himself reminded of the story of "the dog that did not bark," in which a cunning predator conceals himself before suddenly lunging out to fight his victim. Patton wonders if Hitler is playing such a deadly game.

But Patton is conflicted. He knows that the lack of clear-cut intelligence is easily explained. The German army is now based in its own country, rather than in a hostile nation like France. The local citizens are patriots who will not spy on their own soldiers, as the French resistance movement had done so successfully. And because German telephone lines are still largely intact, achieving radio silence is as simple as ordering all military officers to use the telephone instead of the radio. Seen from that perspective, the behavior of the German army is completely logical. The musings of Colonel Oscar Koch might be an exercise in paranoia.

Patton still has every intention of launching Operation Tink on December 19. It will be glorious, starting with the biggest aerial bombardment the Americans have ever poured down on the German army. He finally has the guns and the gas necessary for his tanks and men to make a winter offensive into Germany. With any luck, the war might be over by New Year's Eve after all.

But what if Koch is right? What if there is danger on the Third Army's northern flank?

Finally, Patton stands to leave. He orders that in addition to fine-tuning the last-minute details of Operation Tink, officers plan for emergency measures to rescue First Army should the Germans attack to the north in the Ardennes Forest. If that happens, "our offensive will be called off," he tells his staff. "And we'll have to go up there and save their hides." Koch is most pleased that General Patton wants Third Army to be "in a position to meet whatever happens."

Patton's private sentiments are much more sympathetic. "First Army is making a terrible mistake," he writes in his diary. "It is highly probable the Germans are building up east of them."

But Patton knows he needs to do more than just make backup plans. His concern for the plight of First Army is very real, so he calls General Dwight Eisenhower and passes on Koch's assessment. Ike passes this on to his own G-2, General Kenneth Strong, who relays Patton's concerns to First Army.

Where the warning is promptly ignored.

THE LAST
DESPERATE EFFORT

CHAPTER 6

GERMAN FRONT LINES

DECEMBER 16, 1944 ✠ 5:29 A.M.

SUNRISE IS STILL TWO HOURS away. The morning sky is completely black, without moon or starlight. German artillery crews stand at their guns, making happy small talk and stomping their feet to keep warm. Their cheeks sting from the record December cold. They have been awake for hours, waiting for this moment.

Some day they hope to tell their grandchildren about the great instant when Unternehmen Wacht am Rhein—Operation Watch on the Rhine—began and how they were among the lucky gunners who personally fired the first rounds into the American lines, turning the tide of war in favor of the Fatherland, once and for all. They will tell their descendants about the brilliant deception that allowed a quarter million men, more than seven hundred tanks, and thousands of huge artillery pieces to remain camouflaged in the Ardennes Forest for weeks, giving the German

German soldiers pause to eat as they advance across France. [Mary Evans Picture Library]

attack an element of total surprise. And these young soldiers will talk about the glory of driving through the middle of the area separating the American and British armies, and then the relentless push to reclaim the strategically vital port city of Antwerp. Its capture will allow Adolf Hitler to successfully sue for peace with the west, thereby preserving the Third Reich and preventing an Allied invasion of the German homeland. With the Americans and British neutralized, Hitler will activate step two of Operation Watch on the Rhine and will launch a legendary second attack against Stalin and Russia that defeats the communist Red Army.

That is the story they hope to tell.

But all of that is in the future. Right now these young Germans are eager, awaiting the command to rain down hellfire on their enemies.

At precisely 5:30 A.M. that order is delivered. Up and down the eighty-five-mile German front lines, some sixteen hundred pieces of field artillery open fire. The silent forest explodes, and muzzle blasts light the sky as the furnaces of hell are thrown open. Screaming meemie rockets screech into the darkness, making a deadly sound that American soldiers everywhere find unnerving. And big 88mm guns fire their two-foot-long shells at targets almost ten miles away, hitting U.S. positions before they even know they're being fired upon. Every German soldier within a hundred yards is rendered temporarily deaf from the noise. Hand gestures replace the spoken word.

Otto Skorzeny has never fired an artillery piece in his life, but he has waited for this moment just as eagerly as those men manning the big guns. His life has been a whirlwind since his meeting with the Führer less than two months ago. Operation Greif, as his special role in the offensive is known, has allowed him to scour the ranks of the German military for men who speak fluent English. He has outfitted these men in American uniforms and has captured American tanks, trucks, and jeeps to help them travel effortlessly behind U.S. lines. Their ultimate goal is to make their way through this rugged, snow-covered terrain as quickly as possible to capture three vital bridges over the Meuse River. But their more immediate task is to sow seeds of confusion throughout the American lines. They will spread rumors and misinformation, tear down road signs, and do everything in their power to mislead the Americans as the German army pours into the Ardennes Forest. No lie or act of deception will be overlooked.

The problem facing Skorzeny is that the Americans know all about Operation Greif. Shortly after his Wolf's Lair meeting with Hitler, someone in the German high command circulated a notice up and down the western front: "Secret Commando Operations," the directive stated in bold letters at the top of the page. "The Führer has ordered the formation of a special unit of approximately two battalion strength for commando operations." It went on to ask all English-speaking soldiers, sailors, and

[next pages] *A German antitank company heads to the front in camouflaged vehicles.* [Mary Evans Picture Library]

pilots who wished to volunteer to report to Skorzeny's training center in the town of Friedenthal.

An irate Skorzeny went directly to Hitler to have the notice withdrawn, but the damage was already done. As Skorzeny knew it would, the paper fell into Allied hands. It was the sort of intelligence coup that G-2s like Oscar Koch lived for. And while Skorzeny insisted that Operation Greif be canceled for this blunder, the Führer personally requested that it proceed. Having no choice, Skorzeny reluctantly complied. In the weeks of training that followed, his men lived in a special camp set apart from other German soldiers and were not able to leave. To brush up on their English, they spent time conversing with captured U.S. soldiers and pilots in prisoner of war camps. They learned how to chew gum like Americans, to swear, and to banter using American slang. One soldier who made the mistake of writing home about his whereabouts was immediately shot.

So it is that the sound of the big 75mm guns thundering up and down the lines fills Skorzeny with equal parts euphoria and dread. The legendary commando is known for his ruthlessness, which is just one reason the Allied army has named him the most dangerous man in the German army. But he is also extremely loyal, and fond of his men. As Operation Greif commences, he fusses over them, quietly worrying about their fate. Every mission has peril, but this one is especially dangerous, as every man in Skorzeny's elite commando unit is aware.

If captured by the Americans, they will not be treated as prisoners of war, as regular German soldiers would be.

By disguising themselves as Americans, Skorzeny's men are deliberately violating the Geneva Convention. If captured in German uniforms, they could expect to spend the rest of the war in U.S. captivity, but at least they would live.

But Skorzeny's soldiers will be wearing U.S. uniforms; therefore they will be classified as spies. And as they all know, the punishment for being captured while wearing an enemy uniform is a trial and perhaps death by firing squad.

Skorzeny gives the order to move out.

◆　◆　◆

Confusion reigns. The narrow, muddy roads leading from Germany into the Ardennes are now clogged with German tanks, trucks, horse-drawn carts, and half-tracks as thirty German divisions flood toward the American lines. The front extends north to south through three countries, meaning that German forces are now on the attack in France, Belgium, and Luxembourg. Their movement was supposed to be lightning quick, but speed has not been possible. The biggest surprise attack of the war has become an enormous traffic jam because the roads are too narrow to handle all the German vehicles.

And yet Hitler's gamble is achieving some success. The American army has been caught off guard. Even as German infantry creep through the forest in their winter-white camouflage, the highest levels of Allied leadership still believe that Germany is incapable of launching a major offensive. Some dismiss this as a "spoiling attack"—military jargon for a diversion that weakens the American lines by forcing them to shift men and supplies from some other location. The Ardennes is supposed to be a place to train green troops and a place of rest and sanctuary for soldiers who had been on the front lines too long, chosen because Dwight Eisenhower is convinced that an attack through such wooded and mountainous terrain is impossible. "Of the many pathways that lead to France, the least penetrable is through the Ardennes," notes General Omar Bradley, the commander in charge of the American front lines. "For there the roads are much too scarce, the hills too wooded, and the valleys too limited for maneuver."

Bradley is George Patton's immediate superior, in command of the U.S. forces that stand poised to invade Germany's heartland. Only Dwight Eisenhower has more power among American forces in Europe.

German soldiers load feeder belts holding cartridges into their machine guns. [Mary Evans Picture Library]

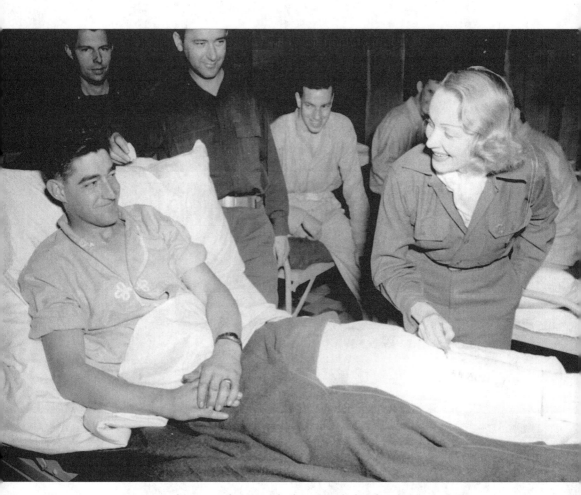

Actress Marlene Dietrich autographs the cast on the leg of Earl E. McFarland at a U.S. hospital in Belgium, where she has been entertaining the GIs.
[Department of Defense, U.S. National Archives]

CHAPTER 7

GENERAL PATTON'S HEADQUARTERS

NANCY, FRANCE ✠ DECEMBER 16, 1944

A s the German offensive in the Ardennes gathers speed, Patton keeps track of events from his headquarters sixty miles south in the town of Nancy. When the time comes that he is called into action, Patton will be taking his orders from Bradley. At the moment, Bradley is caught so unprepared that he has allowed a group of professional American baseball players to tour the area the Germans are now attacking. The famous film actress and singer Marlene Dietrich is also on hand. She has performed in the Belgian crossroads town of Bastogne. Tonight she is scheduled to put on a show for the men of the U.S. Ninety-Ninth Division in the Belgian hamlet of Honsfeld.

That concert is abruptly canceled.

Instead of watching the show, the Ninety-Ninth is digging in, trying desperately to stop the elite German Twelfth and Third SS

Panzer divisions from capturing a spot on the map known as Elsenborn Ridge, a vast, treeless hill that is the picture of natural beauty when wild grasses cover its summit in the summer. But there is no beauty right now. Just frozen mud, corpses, and shell craters. Except for those moments when fog covers the hilltop, or the powerful winds are driving rain and snow into their eyes—which is often—the men of the Ninety-Ninth are in a good position in their foxholes. Any German attack will have to travel a half mile uphill over open ground. Shooting them should be as easy as taking aim and pulling the trigger.

But first they have to see the enemy, and that's not easy. A thick forest nine hundred yards down the slope offers the Germans complete concealment. The woods are dark and gloomy inside, as if covered in a shroud of pines. A dense fog makes the Germans even more invisible. The Ninety-Ninth soldiers are easy targets for the German artillery guns hidden in the forest below—including the high-velocity 88mm guns, which fire a round that travels a half mile per second.

The Ninety-Ninth came to the Ardennes for training, not battle. The men lack winter-camouflaged uniforms, ammunition, and warm clothes, and yet they stand ready to hold the line at all costs.

Because if they don't, Hitler's crazy gamble in the Ardennes just might succeed.

As with the equally strategic nearby location known as the Losheim Gap, the Elsenborn Ridge represents a vital corridor that the German army must possess in order for Operation Watch on the Rhine to accomplish its mission. The Losheim Gap is a narrow valley known to be the pathway for funneling tanks through the rugged Ardennes. The ridge is critical because a network of key roads lies on the other side. Capture the ridge, gain access to the roads, and the German divisions suddenly stand a very good chance of making it all the way to Antwerp.

So the Ninety-Ninth must hold the line. If it fails, Hitler may succeed.

◆   ◆   ◆

Even when the Germans aren't firing, the sounds of their laughter and snippets of conversation carry up the hill to the Ninety-Ninth. The Americans grow depressed and anxious as they hear the never-ending clank of tank treads from the forest, reminding them that the force now gathered down below is indeed an enormous army. In fact, they will learn that the German forces outnumber the Americans by a five-to-one ratio.

As the men await the inevitable, the Ninety-Ninth endures relentless artillery pounding. Those that live to tell the story will long remember the scream of the high-velocity 88mm shells, a sound that gets higher and more pronounced just before impact. They will remember reciting the Lord's Prayer over and over as those assault guns pound their position. They will remember "the filth, the hunger, the cold, and the life of living like an animal."

[next pages] *American soldiers advance through the forest around Bastogne, Belgium, December 26, 1944.* [Mary Evans Picture Library]

And then there is the Ninety-Ninth's new list of unwritten rules: They cannot sleep for any length of time because the German attacks have no set routine. They cannot leave their foxholes during daylight because German gunners zero in on any sign of movement. Many are so cold that they cannot stop shivering.

Over the next four days, the Ninety-Ninth will see 133 more of its men die. Six hundred will fall back to the battalion aid station to be treated for frozen feet. As many as 1,844 will suffer the indignity of going "missing," meaning that their loved ones will never get the closure that comes with having a body to bury.

But the Ninety-Ninth will not quit. And though there are no Germans to their rear, the troops do not fall back. They must hold the line. So they await that inevitable moment when the Germans sprint the half mile up the hillside to kill them. Hour after hour, day after day, in the midst of that endless artillery barrage, they fire back and wait. All the while they wonder whether they will hold the line, get killed in action, or avoid violent death by surrendering.

But like every soldier on both sides of the battlefield, they will soon learn that surrender does not always prevent violent death. In the next three days, Hitler's infantry will murder more than 350 American soldiers and one hundred Belgian civilians.

A German tank unit waits around a fire in the Ardennes. Their camouflaged tank is behind them. [Mary Evans Picture Library]

CHAPTER 8

THE ARDENNES

DECEMBER 17, 1944

A S THE SECOND DAY OF Operation Watch on the Rhine begins, the German First SS Panzer Division is on the move. They are the lead element in the much larger Sixth Panzer Army, tasked with racing through the countryside as quickly as possible to capture three vital bridges over the Meuse River.

The First is the best of the best, a fighting force so highly regarded by Hitler that he has allowed its men to sew his name onto their uniform sleeves. They are all hardened fighters who have seen more than their share of combat in this war. And their armament bears testimony to their elite stature. It's nothing but the finest for the First Panzer: sixty panzer and Panther II tanks, three flak tanks, seventy-five half-tracks, fourteen 20mm guns,

A German soldier guards as vehicles advance to the front. [Mary Evans Picture Library]

twenty-seven 75mm assault guns, and numerous 105mm and 150mm self-propelled howitzers.

In command of this magnificent fighting force is the dashing poster boy for the SS, twenty-nine-year-old Joachim Peiper. "He was approximately five feet eight inches in height, 140 pounds in weight, long dark hair combed straight back, straight well-shaped features," an American prisoner of war will later write.

Peiper was selected to serve as a top assistant for SS leader Hein-rich Himmler, a calculating and brutal man whom Peiper came to idolize. Himmler had been loyal to the *Nationalsozialismus*—National Socialism or Nazi—beliefs of Adolf Hitler long before the Führer achieved power over the German people in 1933. As such, he enjoys Hitler's confidence and has been given the harsh task of carrying out the extermination and suppression of those races, ethnicities, and enemies whom Hitler deems to be a threat to the Reich. Thus Jews, Roma (gypsies), homosexuals, and Nazi politi-cal opponents are sent to concentration camps in Germany and occupied Europe.

Under Himmler's tutelage, Peiper developed the philosophies of intolerance that now guide his military tactics. He stood at Himmler's side to witness the shooting of Polish intellectuals in the early days of the war, and was an eyewitness to the gassing of Jewish civilians, including women and children. When Himmler rewarded Peiper with an assignment to lead a half-track battalion on the Russian front, the fanatical young officer quickly developed a reputation for battlefield brilliance. His men and tanks moved quickly, thrusting and feinting in a manner reminiscent of George S. Patton's lightning-fast maneuvers.

It was Adolf Hitler himself who presented his dashing tank commander with the prestigious Oak Leaves to add to his Knight's Cross, making Peiper the youngest officer in the German army to ever be so honored. As with the commando Otto Skorzeny, Joachim Peiper became the object of the Führer's fascination. Hitler was soon in the habit of rewarding Peiper with not just medals but also the most elite battlefield assignments.

During their time on the Russian front, Peiper's men took few prisoners, believing that the *Untermenschen*—subhumans, as the Germans defined the Russians—did not deserve to live. His men also developed a nickname based on their passion for using fire in battle: the Blowtorch Brigade. On two occasions his tanks completely surrounded Russian villages. His assault troops then set fire to every building, burning to death every single man, woman, and child inside their homes.

Peiper and his men now bring their ruthless talents to Operation Watch on the Rhine, where the need for speed on the battlefield is vital. The Germans must destroy the Allied army before replacements arrive to give the Americans and British a numerical advantage in soldiers and weapons. Thus Peiper and the First are appointed to spearhead the invasion. Since the suicide of Field Marshal Rommel, no other German tank commander can compare to Peiper.

In his final act before Operation Watch on the Rhine launches, Peiper issues orders stating, "There will be no stopping for anything. No booty will be taken, and no enemy vehicles are to be examined. It is not the job of the spearhead to worry about prisoners of war." That would be left to the slower columns of infantry trailing in their wake.

December 17 is a new day for Joachim Peiper and the men of the First Panzer Division. Knowing that overcast skies will keep American fighter-bombers grounded, thus allowing his caravan to move forward unmolested, Peiper races toward the Meuse River.

Just before dawn, Peiper and his men pass through the tiny village of Honsfeld, where they spot American jeeps parked outside a row of local houses. As Peiper presses on to the town of Büllingen, where he knows there is a fuel dump, he leaves the SS infantry behind. They quickly search the houses and emerge with a group of American soldiers, who were literally caught napping. The seventeen men are marched outside, wearing nothing but thin, army-issue boxer shorts. The Americans stand barefoot in the darkness, cursing their fate even as they marvel at the enormity of the German caravan passing before them. Tanks, half-tracks, and trucks curve into the distance as far as the eye can see. Clearly, this is no mere spoiling attack.

Suddenly, SS troopers open fire on the unarmed captured Americans. Sixteen are shot dead where they stand. The remaining

Peiper's troops' most atrocious massacre was at Malmédy, Belgium. Here, U.S. soldiers prepare to remove victims' bodies from the snow. [Granger]

soldier pleads for his life, but the SS takes no pity, murdering him by throwing him in front of a tank.

The news of this and other massacres races up and down the Allied chain of command. The Americans seethe. Although the rules of war make it a crime to kill a man who has surrendered, Peiper's actions make it clear that those rules do not apply to Operation Watch on the Rhine. Many American commanders tell their men that there will be no SS troopers taken prisoner.

If the Germans are not going to comply with the rules of war, then neither will the Americans.

CHAPTER 9

TWELFTH ARMY GROUP HEADQUARTERS

VERDUN, FRANCE ✠ DECEMBER 19, 1944 ✠ 10:30 A.M.

GEORGE S. PATTON IS COLD.

Patton hunkers down in the passenger seat of his open-air jeep, puffing quietly on a cigar. His parka is cinched up tightly around his chin, and he says very little as his driver navigates the streets of this ancient French town. The general ignores the frigid air that has been blasting throughout the ninety-minute drive from his headquarters in Nancy. It is not Patton's way to let the elements affect him.

Patton's driver, Sergeant John Mims of Abbeville, Alabama, slows at the entrance to the old stone barracks serving as Twelfth Army Group headquarters. The sentry snaps to attention and salutes. In return, Patton touches the gloved fingertips of his right hand to his steel helmet. The jeep passes onto a muddy parade ground, and a quick glance at the assembled cars shows that

Dwight Eisenhower and his staff have not yet arrived from Versailles. Nor is Omar Bradley's official vehicle in view. Courtney Hodges, the general in command of the U.S. First Army, is also not in attendance—though this does not surprise Patton. Hodges failed to anticipate the German attack through the Ardennes, and then spent two days denying that it was happening. He even passed the time procuring a new hunting rifle and actually held a raucous staff Christmas party. Hodges was so ashamed of his behavior that he had locked himself in his office, where he sat with arms folded on his desk, head buried in his arms.

General Bradley's behavior hasn't been much better. As recently as two days ago, he was telling an aide that the German's sudden offensive did not concern him.

But Bradley now looks like a fool. The unsettling fact is that the German army has been decimating American forces for the last twelve hours. The situation has led Eisenhower to call an emergency meeting of the top Allied commanders. Patton's Operation Tink is no more. As the irascible general predicted almost two weeks ago, Courtney Hodges and his First Army need to be rescued. And it is Patton's Third Army that will have to do it.

◆　◆　◆

"The present situation is to be regarded as one of opportunity for us and not of disaster," Dwight Eisenhower tells the crowd of generals and senior officers seated at the long conference table. Ike has just been notified that he has been promoted to five-star general. But rather than showing elation, his face is pale and tired. A look

General Eisenhower (left) meets with Generals Patton, Bradley, and Hodges on an airfield in Germany, March 1945. [Bridgeman Art Library]

around the dank second-floor room shows that every top commander, with the exception of British Field Marshal Montgomery and Lieutenant General Courtney Hodges, is in attendance. A situation map sits on an easel. The air smells of Patton's cigar, wet wool, and wood smoke from the fire burning in a potbellied stove. The low flame fails to warm the room, and almost no one has removed his thick overcoat.

Eisenhower continues, forcing a smile, "There will be only cheerful faces at this conference table."

"Hell," Patton interrupts, "let's have the guts to let the sons of bitches go all the way to Paris. Then we'll really cut 'em off and chew 'em up."

Patton's brash remarks fail to get much more than a grim chuckle. But they set a tone. Patton's aggressiveness is vital to Allied success. For while everyone else in the cold, damp room might have a vague idea of how to rescue the First Army, there is little doubt that the job will fall to Patton.

"George, that's fine," Eisenhower responds, once again reclaiming the room. "But the enemy must never be allowed to cross the Meuse."

This is the line in the sand. Joachim Peiper and his SS panzers are desperate to reach the Meuse River and secure its bridges in order to advance the German attack, but the Allies cannot let this happen.

Eisenhower's G-2 intelligence chief, the British Major General Kenneth Strong, briefs the room on the current location of the

American and German forces. Since late September, the German army has successfully prevented the U.S. and British forces from making any significant advances into the Fatherland. The war has become a stalemate. The Allies foolishly rested on their laurels, assuming the Germans could never reverse the tide. That was a mistake.

If the seventeen divisions of German soldiers now marching through the Ardennes can somehow make it across the Meuse, the war could change radically—and not in the Allies' favor.

"George," Eisenhower states. "I want you to command this move—under Brad's supervision, of course." Here Eisenhower nods at Omar Bradley.

Ike continues, "A counterattack with at least six divisions. When can you start?"

Patton is ready. He has not only come to the meeting equipped with three different battle plans, but he met earlier this morning with his staff and arranged a simple series of code words. Launching Third Army's attack is as simple as Patton calling his headquarters and saying the code for whichever plan is chosen.

"As soon as you're through with me," Patton replies.

"When can you attack?" Eisenhower presses.

"The morning of December 21, with three divisions," Patton responds, still clutching his lighted cigar.

The room lapses into embarrassed silence. Patton has named a date only two days away. These career military officers know to be diplomatic when a man makes a fool of himself. And Patton has clearly crossed that line. Three divisions is not a small, nimble fighting force. It is a slow-moving colossus, spread out over miles of front lines. The idea that one hundred thousand men plus supplies can somehow be uprooted and moved one hundred miles in forty-eight hours is ludicrous. If the men make it but the guns and gasoline don't, all is lost. Attempting such an impossible task in the dead of winter, on narrow and icy roads, borders on the impossible. As they have seen before, Patton's big mouth appears to be his undoing.

Eisenhower has seen this play out one too many times. "Don't be fatuous, George."

Patton looks to his deputy chief of staff, Colonel Paul Harkins. Nothing is said, but Harkins nods, confirming that Patton is standing on solid ground.

"We can do that," says Patton, staring straight into Eisenhower's eyes.

Charles Codman, Patton's aide-de-camp, will later write of "a stir, a shuffling of feet, as those present straightened up in their chairs. In some faces, skepticism. But through the room, the current of excitement leaped like a flame."

Patton seizes the moment. Stepping to the map, he points out German weaknesses. This goes on for an hour. Omar Bradley says very little, realizing that this operation belongs to Patton—and Patton alone.

Finally, as the meeting breaks up, Eisenhower jokes with his old friend. "Funny thing, George, every time I get a new star, I get attacked."

"Yes," Patton shoots back. "And every time you get attacked, I bail you out."

◆　◆　◆

But this time, Patton might be too late. Rapid response is vital to stopping the Nazi penetration. In military terms, the blast hole that has been created in the Allied lines is known as a salient. American newspapers are simply calling it "the bulge." In America, the Battle of the Bulge has shocked the public. The siege of a particular town in the middle of the bulge, Bastogne, is becoming a symbol of holding out against impossible odds.

[next pages] *SS infantry advance in the Ardennes, December 1944.* [Bridgeman Art Library]

CHAPTER 10

BASTOGNE, BELGIUM

DECEMBER 19, 1944

B RIGADIER GENERAL ANTHONY MCAULIFFE IS racing toward the town of Werbomont, fighting his way through the tides of U.S. soldiers retreating in shock at the death and devastation they have survived. These shattered soldiers are clear evidence that the Germans are hardly defeated. They are aggressively ruthless and have already slaughtered thousands of Americans in just four days.

McAuliffe is leading fresh troops, the 101st Airborne Division, into battle, although they are several miles behind him. He is traveling in a caravan made up of almost four hundred vehicles. Many of the drivers are black Americans, members of the old Red Ball Express. They drive with their headlights blazing, which is usually forbidden in a combat zone but now allows them to travel at a quicker speed. Normally that would be disastrous, as the

American soldiers on the way to relieve their comrades in Bastogne.
[Mary Evans Picture Library]

paratroopers would be butchered from the air, their silhouettes standing out in the snowy fields beside the roads, completely visible to Nazi pilots. But the calculated gamble is paying off. The Luftwaffe is not flying tonight.

As he endures the bitter cold in a rock-hard passenger seat, McAuliffe is well aware that the more than eleven thousand paratroopers of the 101st are spoiling for a fight.

They have no choice: They are the last line of American defense. There are no reinforcements. Should the Germans defeat the 101st at Werbomont, there will be no reserves waiting to stop them.

But Brigadier General Tony McAuliffe, West Point class of 1918, never makes it to Werbomont. Nor does the 101st Airborne.

Instead, they are suddenly diverted to a tiny hamlet that is no more than a speck on the Ardennes map. The Germans call the village "road octopus" because seven different highways sprout in seven different directions from its center. They see the key to success in Operation Watch on the Rhine as gaining control of the local roads, which will allow their heavy tanks to travel more quickly. So, the Germans covet this town.

The road octopus is more commonly known as Bastogne.

Until a few days ago, McAuliffe had never heard of it. But now, for better or worse, he is here. As his jeep finally roars into the town center, he finds a miserable scenario. The power and water

Brigadier General Tony McAuliffe (left). [Associated Press]

supply has been cut off. The town square is choked with refugees and carts piled high with their possessions. German shelling has begun to reduce much of Bastogne to rubble.

Yet McAuliffe must defend this horrible little burg at all costs. He sets up his command post in the basement of the Hotel de Commerce, across the street from the train station, and impatiently awaits the arrival of his troops. A quick glance at the situation map boards tacked up along the compound walls show how desperately the Germans want to capture Bastogne: They have committed three divisions and parts of four more. McAuliffe's eleven thousand paratroopers, and an additional armored division numbering three thousand seventy-five soldiers and tanks, are on the verge of being surrounded by a force of fifty-five thousand German fighters and tanks. Once the Germans close the noose, there will be no way for the Americans to escape.

Lieutenant General Troy Middleton, McAuliffe's immediate superior, briefs him before leaving.

"But don't worry," Middleton emphasizes. "Help is on the way from Patton."

With that, Middleton hurries to his staff car and quickly drives out of town, knowing the Germans are just two miles away.

CHAPTER 11

BASTOGNE, BELGIUM

DECEMBER 22, 1944

McAULIFFE IS EXHAUSTED. HE BARELY slept last night because the German air force bombed Bastogne, with one blast almost destroying his command post in the basement of the hotel. Just before noon he steals away to a small, quiet room, zips himself into his sleeping bag, and naps. His staff knows to wake him if anything of importance occurs.

Meanwhile, in the meadows and forests ringing Bastogne, the men of the 101st have actually turned being surrounded into a tactically positive situation. They keep their perimeter tight, facing outward, waiting for the German attack.

About noon on December 22, 1944, it is quiet enough for some of the men of the 327th Glider Regiment to actually stand outside their foxholes on the Kessler family farm south of Bastogne, making small talk.

A most odd sight then presents itself: Marching toward them are four German soldiers, carrying a white flag as large as a bed-sheet. They walk into the American lines fearlessly, even strolling past a bazooka team on the outer perimeter without hesitation. The men of F Company shoulder their M-1 carbines, but the Germans keep coming. "This doesn't make sense," says one American, wondering why the Germans appear to be surrendering.

Three American soldiers walk cautiously up the road to greet the Germans. They soon stand face-to-face with two officers and two enlisted men. The officers wear polished black boots and long, warm overcoats. One of them, the short, stocky lieutenant, carries a briefcase.

The Americans never take their fingers off the triggers of their M-1 rifles, unsure if this is a trick.

It is not.

In fact, it is a gesture on the part of German General Heinrich Lüttwitz, commander of the forces surrounding Bastogne, that is both gallant and arrogant. He thinks it absurd to slaughter so many brave American soldiers. Instead, Lüttwitz is offering Tony McAuliffe and the 101st a chance to save their own lives by surrendering. War being war, however, should the Americans refuse to throw down their weapons, Lüttwitz will order that Bastogne be leveled and every American soldier annihilated. There will be no prisoners.

An SS patrol in the Ardennes, 1945. [Mary Evans Picture Library]

Soon enough, news of the note is passed up the chain of command. Within an hour, Tony McAuliffe is being awakened to the news that a German surrender demand is making its way to headquarters.

"Nuts," he mutters, still half asleep.

"They want to surrender?" McAuliffe asks, taking the note from Lieutenant Colonel Ned Moore, his chief of staff.

"No, sir," Moore corrects him. "They want *us* to surrender."

McAuliffe laughs and begins to read.

The letter is dated December 22, 1944.

To the U.S.A. Commander of the encircled town of Bastogne.

The fortune of war is changing. This time the U.S.A. forces in and near Bastogne have been encircled by strong German armored units. More German armored units have crossed the river Ourthe near Ortheuville, have taken Marche and reached St. Hubert by passing through Hompre-Sibret-Tillet. Libramont is in German hands. There is only one possibility to save the encircled U.S.A. troops from total annihilation: that is the honorable surrender of the encircled town. In order to think it over a term of two hours will be granted beginning with the presentation of this note.

If this proposal should be rejected, one German Artillery Corps and six heavy A.A. battalions are ready

*to annihilate the U.S.A. troops in and near Bastogne.
The order for firing will be given immediately after this
two hours' term.*

*All the serious civilian losses caused by this artillery fire
would not correspond with the well known American
humanity.*

The German Commander

McAuliffe looks at his staff. "Well, I don't know what to tell
them."

"That first remark of yours would be hard to beat," replies Lieutenant Colonel Harry Kinnard, in his Texas twang.

"What do you mean?" McAuliffe responds.

"Sir, you said, 'nuts,' " answers his chief of operations.

McAuliffe mulls it over. He knows his history and suspects this
moment will become famous. One French general refused to surrender at the Battle of Waterloo with the far more crass response
of "merde."

And so the message is quickly typed: "To the German Commander, Nuts! The American Commander."

When the letter is presented to the German emissaries, they
don't understand. "What is this, 'nuts'?"

Colonel Joseph Harper, regimental commander of the 327th,
who delivered McAuliffe's response, illuminates them. "It means
you can go to hell." He adds, "And I'll tell you something else.

If you continue to attack, we will kill every goddamn German that tries to break into this city."

The Germans snap to attention and salute. "We will kill many Americans. This is war."

"On your way, bud," replies Harper.

◆　◆　◆

Rumors and innuendo spread throughout the army. There is a rumor that C-47s are going to airdrop precious supplies of food and bullets into Bastogne. And the men are hearing that George S. Patton is sending an armored division to bail them out. Maybe two divisions. But they can't be sure of this.

In fact, at the moment Patton is asking for help from another source.

CHAPTER 12

FONDATION PESCATORE

LUXEMBOURG CITY, LUXEMBOURG ✠ DECEMBER 23, 1944 ✠ 9 A.M.

GEORGE S. PATTON TAKES OFF HIS helmet as he enters the Catholic chapel. Though Episcopalian, he is in need of a place to worship. His boots echo on the stone floor as he walks reverently to the foot of the altar. The scent of melting wax from the many votive candles fills the small chamber. Patton kneels, unfolding the prayer he has written for this occasion, and bows his head.

"Sir, this is Patton talking," he says, speaking candidly to the Almighty. "The past fourteen days have been straight hell. Rain, snow, more rain, more snow—and I am beginning to wonder what's going on in Your headquarters. Whose side are You on anyway?"

Patton and the Third Army are now thirty-three miles south of Bastogne. Every available man under his command has joined the race to rescue the city. The bulge in the American lines is sixty miles deep and thirty miles wide, with Bastogne an American island in the center. And while Patton's men have so far been successful in maintaining their steady advance, there is still widespread doubt that he can succeed. Outnumbered and outgunned by the Germans, Patton faces the daunting challenge of attacking on icy roads in thick snow, with little air cover.

So the general prays.

> *For three years my chaplains have been telling me that this is a religious war. This, they tell me, is the Crusades all over again, except that we're riding tanks instead of chargers. They insist that we are here to annihilate the Germans and the godless Hitler so that religious freedom may return to Europe. Up until now I have gone along with them, for You have given us Your unreserved cooperation. Clear skies and a calm sea in Africa made the landings highly successful and helped us to eliminate Rommel. Sicily was comparatively easy and You supplied excellent weather for the armored dash across France, the greatest military victory that You have thus far allowed me. You have often given me excellent guidance in difficult command situations and You have led German units into traps that made their elimination fairly simple.*
>
> *But now You've changed horses midstream. You seem to have given von Rundstedt [German field marshal and Hitler's commander in chief on the western front] every break in the book, and frankly, he's beating the hell out of*

us. My army is neither trained nor equipped for winter warfare. And as You know, this weather is more suitable for Eskimos than for southern cavalrymen.

But now, Sir, I can't help but feel that I have offended You in some way. That suddenly You have lost all sympathy for our cause. That You are throwing in with von Rundstedt and his paper-hanging god [Hitler]. You know without me telling You that our situation is desperate. Sure, I can tell my staff that everything is going according to plan, but there's no use telling You that my 101st Airborne is holding out against tremendous odds in Bastogne, and that this continual storm is making it impossible to supply them even from the air. I've sent Hugh Gaffey, one of my ablest generals, with his Fourth Armored Division north toward that all-important road center to relieve the encircled garrison, and he's finding Your weather more difficult than he is the Krauts.

This isn't the first time Patton has resorted to divine intervention. Every man in the Third Army now carries a three-by-five card that has a Christmas greeting from Patton on one side and a special prayer for good weather on the other. He firmly believes that faith is vital when it comes to doing the impossible. And even though he has given the cruel order that all SS soldiers are to be shot rather than taken prisoner, Patton sees no theological conflict in asking God to allow him to kill the enemy.

Patton continues:

> *I don't like to complain unreasonably, but my soldiers*
> *from Meuse to Echternach are suffering tortures of the*
> *damned. Today I visited several hospitals, all full of*
> *frostbite cases, and the wounded are dying in the fields*
> *because they cannot be brought back for medical care.*

Patton's prayer is clear. Not only is he asking for deliverance, he is asking for power. Few men are ever given the chance to change the course of history so completely. No one, not even Dwight Eisenhower, is standing in Patton's way. If the men inside Bastogne are to be rescued, it will be because of the brilliance of George S. Patton—as he himself knows. But to succeed, he will need a little help from above.

The last words of Patton's prayer are for the ages.

> *Damn it, Sir, I can't fight a shadow. Without Your*
> *cooperation from a weather standpoint, I am deprived of*
> *accurate disposition of the German armies and how in the*
> *hell can I be intelligent in my attack? All of this probably*
> *sounds unreasonable to You, but I have lost all patience*
> *with Your chaplains who insist that this is a typical*
> *Ardennes winter, and that I must have faith.*
>
> *Faith and patience be damned! You have just got to*
> *make up Your mind whose side You are on. You must come to*

my assistance, so that I may dispatch the entire German army as a birthday present to Your Prince of Peace.

Sir, I have never been an unreasonable man; I am not going to ask You to do the impossible. I do not even insist upon a miracle, for all I request is four days of clear weather.

Give me four days so that my planes can fly, so that my fighter bombers can bomb and strafe, so that my reconnaissance may pick out targets for my magnificent artillery. Give me four days of sunshine to dry this blasted mud, so that my tanks roll, so that ammunition and rations may be taken to my hungry, ill-equipped infantry. I need these four days to send von Rundstedt and his godless army to their Valhalla. I am sick of this unnecessary butchering of American youth, and in exchange for four days of fighting weather, I will deliver You enough Krauts to keep Your bookkeepers months behind in their work.

Amen.

Head bowed, Patton continues to pray while Sergeant John Mims waits outside with his jeep. When the general is ready, they will set out for yet another day prowling the roads of the Ardennes Forest. Without planes to offer overhead reconnaissance, Patton must see the battle lines for himself.

Their travels also serve another purpose. Patton seeks out American forces wherever he can, exhorting his troops as they march in long columns up the snowy farm roads. Tanks and trucks travel

round the clock toward Bastogne. The infantry wear long greatcoats. The tank commanders ride with their chests and shoulders poking out of top hatches, faces swaddled in thick wool scarves. The heavy snow covering the roads, forests, and farmlands covers their vehicles and mutes the rumble of engines, giving Third Army's advance a ghostly feel. But it can also lead to death: Unable to distinguish which snow-covered tanks are American Shermans and which are German panzers, some U.S. P-47 Thunderbolt pilots will make the cruel mistake of bombing their own.

Patton is a relentless presence in his open-air vehicle, red-faced and blue-lipped as Sergeant Mims fearlessly weaves through the long column of tanks and trucks. Patton is frozen from the cold air as he rides

General Patton rides in his customary open-air jeep. [Mary Evans Picture Library]

to the front lines to rally his men. "I spent five or six hours almost every day in an open car," as he will later write in his journal about his zeal to be in the thick of the action. "I never had a cold, and my face, though sometimes slightly blistered, did not hurt me much. . . ."

Just yesterday, a column of the Fourth Armored Division that was advancing on Bastogne was shocked to see Patton get out of his jeep and help the soldiers push a vehicle out of a snowdrift. The men of the Third Army are bolstered by Patton's constant presence. They speak of him warmly, with nicknames like The Old Man and Georgie. His willingness to put himself in harm's way and endure the freezing conditions has many American soldiers now believing the general would never ask them to do something he wouldn't do himself.

CHAPTER 13

ADLERHORST

LANGENHAIN-ZIEGENBERG, GERMANY
DECEMBER 24, 1944 ✠ 1 P.M.

THE MAN WITH 127 DAYS to live can barely see.

The sun shines brightly on Adolf Hitler's pale, exhausted face as he stares up at more than one thousand Allied fighter-bombers that have come to destroy the Fatherland on Christmas Eve. The Führer stands 123 miles east of where Patton knelt to pray, ensconced in a drab bunker complex known as the Adler-horst, and the drone of the bombers has pulled him out of the dining room of Haus 1. As his lunch grows cold, Hitler surveys the danger above him.

"*Mein* Führer," gasps Christa Schroeder, his personal secretary, "we have lost the war, haven't we?"

Hitler assures her that this is not the case. So even as the B-17 Flying Fortresses and B-24 Liberators continue their deadly

journey into the German heartland, Hitler saunters back inside to eat, passing a well-decorated Christmas tree that will soon be lit by candlelight.

The Führer's physical condition has continued to deteriorate from his drugged, highly stressful life. His unstable gait is that of an old man. Lunch is his usual fare of vegetables and fruit— asparagus and peppers are personal favorites—served with salad and rice. A dozen female food tasters have already sampled the fare to ensure that Hitler is not poisoned. Hitler is barely strong enough to hold the fork with his right hand, which has grown so weak that he can no longer sign official documents— leaving his staff to forge his signature.

Hitler's left hand is even worse. He cannot stop its palsied shakes, and so it now rests in his lap. The Führer eats mechanically, even leaning his head over the plate to shovel the vegetables in faster. He runs his right index finger along his short black mustache between bites. The Führer absentmindedly chews his nails; his table manners, in the words of one witness, "are little short of shocking."

The Führer has been holed up in the Adlerhorst since before Operation Watch on the Rhine began and directs the battle from this secret fortress. The elaborate collection of seven houses is actually a cleverly concealed military command post. Nestled in the crags of the Taunus Mountains, the Adlerhorst was built in the

Bombs explode on Berlin's industrial area. This photograph was taken by one of the bombers. [Mary Evans Picture Library]

shadow of the medieval Castle Kransberg, which shields the Eagle's Eyrie from prying eyes. Each building appears to be an innocent German cottage, with wood exteriors and interior furnishings of deer antlers and paintings depicting hunting scenes.

But the walls are actually reinforced concrete, three feet thick. Antiaircraft guns are hidden in the surrounding forest, where Hitler takes his morning strolls with Blondi. It is to the Adlerhorst that Hitler brought his top generals on December 11 to lay out his counterattack strategy. In the underground situation room of Haus 2, an elated Hitler celebrated the operation's opening success on December 16. He was so overjoyed that he couldn't sleep—a condition no doubt enhanced by injections of glucose, iron, and vitamin B from Dr. Morell.

In the eight days since the offensive into the Ardennes began, Hitler has had much to cheer. His favorite commando, Otto Skorzeny, and the men of Operation Greif successfully roamed behind American lines, spreading lies and innuendo that caused widespread panic. A few of Skorzeny's commandos were caught and swiftly shot by firing squads for the war crime of disguising themselves in enemy uniforms. But by then the damage was done.

GIs everywhere became jittery as news of German soldiers wearing American uniforms and speaking English spread up and down the Allied chain of command. U.S. soldiers became distrustful of any and all strangers. Cases of mistaken identity led

Hitler and Eva Braun in 1938. [Mary Evans Picture Library]

Americans to shoot other Americans. Vehicles passing through military checkpoints were halted, and the occupants were asked to prove their nationality by answering questions about American culture that only a real GI would know.

Those who did not realize the difference between baseball's American and National leagues or know the name of actress Betty Grable's last motion picture were often taken into custody. An American brigadier general who thought the Chicago Cubs were in the American League was placed under arrest and held at gunpoint for five hours. British Field Marshal Bernard Montgomery refused to answer questions, then ordered his driver to speed through a checkpoint, at which time the American guards shot out his tires.

When British film actor-turned-soldier David Niven was unable to recall who had won the 1940 World Series, he answered, "Haven't the faintest idea. But I do know I made a picture with Ginger Rogers in 1938."

The sentry let him pass.

So great was the Skorzeny-induced hysteria that Dwight Eisenhower was placed under around-the-clock protection after one captured German commando confessed that Skorzeny planned to assassinate Eisenhower.

In the end, the damage done by Operation Greif was intense but

A captured German soldier is found in possession of a pair of American army pants. [Mary Evans Picture Library]

did not change the course of the actual battle. Even the flamboyant Skorzeny admitted his subterfuge could not turn the tide.

◆　◆　◆

Hitler paces around his underground command post, staring at the battle maps spread atop the long rectangular conference table. He stops now and then to nibble on the molasses-filled ginger pastry that temporarily appeases his insatiable sweet tooth. What he desperately longs to hear is some good news from the front. Instead, he hears that Bastogne has not yet fallen, and that the Second SS Panzer Division is just three miles from the Meuse River but has run out of fuel and can go no farther. Rather than waging war, the Second SS Panzer now hides in the forest, desperately covering its stalled vehicles with tree branches and heaps of snow to camouflage them from the American P-47 Thunderbolts that prowl the Ardennes sky.

But perhaps the most crushing blow is the fate of Hitler's great tank commander, Joachim Peiper, and the men of the elite First SS Panzer Division.

Peiper has been trapped in the small village of La Gleize, just two bridges away from crossing the Meuse River, and spearheading a fatal thrust through the Allied lines toward Antwerp. For three days Peiper has been using what little ammunition he has left to fend off American artillery and tank attacks.

General Kurt Zietzler and General Joachim Rouff aid Hitler in devising strategy. [Mary Evans Picture Library]

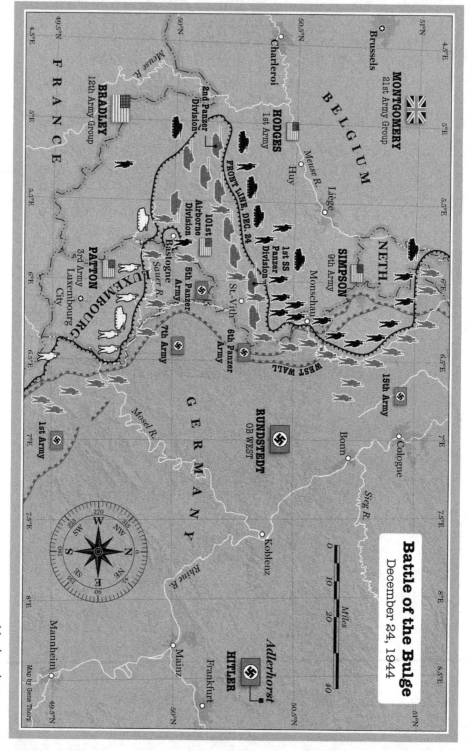

Battle of the Bulge
December 24, 1944

Map by Gene Thorp

Map legend is on page x.

A German panzer usually carried a crew of five men. [Mary Evans Picture Library]

◆ ◆ ◆

Colonel Peiper does not want his men to die. Thus he hatches a daring plan that may give hope to a hopeless situation.

Just after 5 P.M. on December 23, Joachim Peiper radioes German headquarters and asks permission to destroy his twenty-eight remaining tanks and escape on foot.

The request is denied. The Führer refuses any defensive action.

Later that night, Peiper once again pleads for the lives of his eight hundred remaining men, arguing that the only way to save them is to flee through the woods.

Again, permission is denied.

A furious Peiper unholsters his pistol and fires several shots into the radio. The explosion mirrors the depth of his frustration.

Peiper makes up his mind. The First Panzer must escape, even if it means disobeying a direct order.

The word is passed.

By 3 A.M. on December 24, Peiper and every tank crew member in the First gather to do something they have not done on a battlefield for a very long time—walk. Tank commanders throughout the division struggle to maintain their stoicism as they leave behind the fighting machines that have given them the godlike power of life and death for one thrilling and sleepless week. A dozen miles and two river crossings lie between Peiper and the German lines. The plan is to travel through woods by night and remain hidden during the day to avoid being spotted by those dreaded American Thunderbolt pilots.

German tanks. [Alamy]

Although the Nazi Party de-emphasized religion, traditional Christmas decorations were put up in homes, including Hitler's. [Mary Evans Picture Library]

The First forms a long, single-file column and begins its march in complete silence. A skeleton crew remains behind to blow up the now useless panzers and half-tracks. The spearhead of Operation Watch on the Rhine is no longer moving forward. The First SS Panzer Division is in full retreat, the burning hulls of its tanks lighting up the wintry Christmas Eve sky.

◆ ◆ ◆

The Holy Evening, as Christmas Eve is known throughout Germany, ends late for Adolf Hitler. It is actually 4 A.M. on Christmas Day as he slowly ascends the stairs from his war room and readies himself for bed. Christmas doesn't have a special meaning for Hitler. He refuses to acknowledge any religious aspect of the day even though he was brought up by devoutly Roman Catholic parents. Rising at noon, Hitler receives the news that Peiper and his division have escaped entrapment. This morning, as Hitler lay sleeping, 770 men of the eight hundred who began the journey from La Gleize swam the icy Salm River and reached the German lines safely.

That evening, after dressing in his usual formal manner, Hitler meets with his staff to celebrate the holiday, drinking a rare glass of wine and making jovial small talk. Then he descends once again into his war room. He seeks the latest reports from Bastogne, certain that he can renew his stalled attack if he captures the road octopus. Despite his declining physical condition, there is a gleam in Hitler's eye as he scrutinizes the maps. It is a gleam that his generals know well, for it is how the Führer looks when he is devising some brilliant way to outwit his enemies.

No matter what the Allies might think, Adolf Hitler is far from beaten.

Dead bodies and destroyed vehicles litter a street in Bastogne, December 1944.
[Mary Evans Picture Library]

CHAPTER 14

THIRD ARMY HEADQUARTERS

LUXEMBOURG CITY, LUXEMBOURG ✠ DECEMBER 26, 1944 ✠ 2 P.M.

GEORGE S. PATTON IS TIRED OF breaking his promises. The air in his palatial headquarters is thick with cigarette smoke and the clack of typewriters. Junior officers and enlisted subordinates make sure to keep their distance from the volatile general as they range in and out of the situation room, not wanting to incur the wrath of a clearly exhausted Patton. When a message arrives from Eisenhower stating that he is very anxious that Patton put every effort on securing Bastogne, Patton nearly explodes.

"What the hell does he think I've been doing for the last week?" Patton will write in his diary tonight, after taking the professional high road and not criticizing his boss in front of the headquarters staff. After all, he has covered seventy-one miles in the past week, more than half the distance from Nancy to Bastogne.

Privately Patton seethes at Eisenhower's tactical choices. The

Seventeenth Airborne, Eleventh Armored Division, and Eighty-Seventh Infantry have all been moved one hundred miles back to the French city of Reims as reserves, just in case the German breakthrough goes even deeper into the American lines. "We should attack," he complains to his staff. Patton could sorely use the additional firepower those units would bring to the relief of Bastogne. Instead, they sit in the patient defensive mode that Patton deplores.

"We should attack."

The general broods and studies maps of the front lines. He promised General Anthony McAuliffe and the 101st Airborne that he would be in Bastogne on Christmas Day. He even sent a message, promising them a special Christmas present. But that did not happen. Instead, Patton's tank crews are spread out over a thirty-mile-wide front, locked in a stalemate. They are gaining little ground and losing too many men and tanks as they battle for each and every inch of Belgian soil.

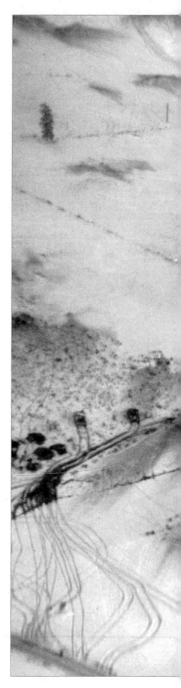

Tanks and infantry of the U.S. 6th Armored Division advance toward Bastogne. [Mary Evans Picture Library]

Gone is the lightning speed of just days ago, when Patton's forces raced into combat like the cavalry. Thousands of dead Americans now lie frozen in the fields outside Bastogne, their faces turned the color of red wine from the blood pooling after death. Patton keeps a detailed tally of Allied and German casualties in his journal and knows that Germans are dying in far greater numbers.

He also knows that casualties tell only part of the story. The German lines are holding fast. Patton and the Third Army are stuck. Tony McAuliffe and the 101st Airborne are now enduring yet another day in the violent hellhole of Bastogne.

The soldiers and the three thousand civilians who share Bastogne are reluctant to leave their cellars for any reason. Elsewhere in the city, American wounded lie atop squalid litters inside makeshift field hospitals. They cannot help but hear the rasp of the bone saw as army surgeons cut away the destroyed arms and legs of their fellow soldiers.

George S. Patton relishes war. He accepts that horrible death can happen to any man, at any time. Patton finds war glorious and thinks there is no finer test of a man's courage.

Yet he is not immune to human suffering. Thus the Battle of the Bulge is taking a hard toll on Patton. It is within his power to ease the pain and hardship of those embattled men of the 101st Airborne. His failure to do so haunts him.

It has been a week since the meeting with Eisenhower in Verdun. Patton is too keyed up to sleep more than a few hours every night. So he is drained and dog-tired. His face is burned bright red from the windblast of too many hours in his open-air jeep. The lines around his blue eyes are deep. "I saw a tired, aging man," notes a Red Cross volunteer who caught a glimpse of Patton at a Christmas Eve church service. "A sorrowful, solitary man, a lonely man, with veiled eyes behind which there was going on a torment of brooding and depression."

Patton cannot rest. He is failing. "Christmas dawned cold and clear," he wrote in his journal yesterday. "Lovely weather for killing Germans—although the thought seemed somewhat at variance with the spirit of the day."

There was no Christmas truce, as so often occurred during World War I. So Patton arranged for every man in his army to have a turkey dinner—cold sandwiches for soldiers at the front, a hot meal for those behind the lines—and he left early in the morning to visit every one of his combat divisions.

It was a long day, and Patton was not uplifted by what he saw.

Now he spends December 26 knowing that some of his tanks are within a half dozen miles of Bastogne. But today, as with yesterday and the day before, victory hardly seems likely. Reports filtering back to his headquarters state that Patton's tank divisions continue to take heavy casualties.

Making matters worse—far worse—is that rather than helping Patton by pushing his own army south toward Bastogne, British Field Marshal Montgomery refuses to attack. He says his army is not ready.

◆   ◆   ◆

The phone rings in Patton's headquarters. Major General Hugh Gaffey, commander of the Fourth Armored Division, is on the other end, requesting permission to launch a high-risk attack into Bastogne immediately.

Patton does not hesitate. "I told him to go ahead," he will write in his journal tonight. With that order, the Fourth Armored Division begins fighting its way toward Tony McAuliffe and the trapped men of the 101st Airborne.

Lieutenant Colonel Creighton "Abe" Abrams commands the spearhead Thirty-Seventh Tank Battalion of the Fourth Armored. He chews on an unlit cigar so enormous that his men compare it to the barrel of a gun. Perched atop a hill, Abrams sits tall in the turret hatch of his Sherman tank, nicknamed Thunderbolt VII. He has already had six Shermans shot out from under him—all named Thunderbolt. In September he was awarded the Distinguished Service Cross for courage under fire. The men love him because he is a lax disciplinarian away from the battlefield and knows there is a time and place for fun. But when it comes time to fight, they also know they are expected to do precisely as their commanding officer orders.

Bastogne lies just a few miles away. A line of twenty Shermans, the survivors of his original fifty-three, snakes down the narrow and rutted country road behind Abrams. These tanks have names, too, such as Cobra King, Tonto, Deuces Wild, Betty, and Destruction.

The M4 General Sherman tank was the model most widely used during World War II by U.S., British, Canadian, and Free French forces. [Mary Evans Picture Library]

Scanning the horizon with his high-powered binoculars, Abrams watches hundreds of C-47 cargo planes dropping supplies to the besieged men of Bastogne. Parachutes laden with ammo, food, and medical supplies blossom against the leaden sky, but Abrams also sees that German antiaircraft fire is successfully shooting down many of the slow-moving twin-engine supply planes. They spiral to earth, soon to explode, the pilots consigned to a fiery death.

The sight of the airdrop, along with the knowledge that American soldiers have been suffering and dying inside Bastogne for more than a week, fills Abrams with a sense of urgency. He sees the 101st defenders crouched down in their snowy foxholes outside the town. He also knows that hundreds of hidden Germans are waiting to destroy any rescuing force.

But Lieutenant Colonel Abrams is convinced he and his men can get through.

So Abrams orders an all-out blitz on the tiny hamlets of Clochimont and Assenois, which sit between him and Bastogne. If he takes the villages, Abrams can be in Bastogne within hours. But if the effort fails, his small force will surely be wiped out. The narrow road he plans to use could become a death trap.

All available American artillery in the area launch an

American soldiers quickly dig foxholes as German fire opens up. A dead soldier lies in the foreground. [Mary Evans Picture Library]

[next pages] *In position during the Battle of the Bulge, 15mm "Long Tom" field guns fire shells to a distance of thirteen miles.* [Mary Evans Picture Library]

immediate barrage to soften the German defenses. The thunder of 155mm guns booms across the Belgian countryside as shell after shell lands on German positions in the forests and villages. In all, more than two thousand rounds will fall on the German fighters today.

"We're going to get to those people," Abrams commands. He waves his arms high in the air, and his tanks churn forward.

There is nothing quick about their movement. The Sherman's top speed is just twenty-four miles per hour. Nor is there any level of cover. Thanks to the artillery barrage, the Germans know the Americans are coming. They can now clearly see Abrams and his line of Shermans and half-track armor steering down the hill into Clochimont.

Abrams closes the hatch and conceals himself inside the three-inch-thick steel of the turret as Shermans burst through Clochimont's ancient town square. Nothing must stop them. German artillery explodes all around. One shell knocks down a telephone pole, blocking the road and bringing the column to a lurching halt.

The pole has to be moved.

Abrams and several other men immediately climb out of their tanks. With sniper fire pinging off steel and glancing off the rutted road, they work as a team to swing the heavy log out of the way.

Then it's back into their Shermans. Behind them, a column of infantry secures Clochimont and will stay there until the mopping up is complete. A second column of foot soldiers travels with Abrams's tanks as they move toward the concealed German positions alongside the road through Assenois.

Rather than simply race through the town, Abrams chooses to level it. Every building that might hide a German becomes a target. The Shermans do not stop firing, loading, and shooting their big 75mm and 76mm guns—as many as seven times per minute. Meanwhile, infantrymen ruthlessly hunt down Germans, screaming "Come out!" to induce them to surrender.

The battle in the forests surrounding Assenois will continue long into the night, but by afternoon it is clear that the Americans have carved a small channel through the German lines. The path is less than one quarter of a mile wide, and Germans are poised on both sides, prepared to counterattack and once again close the road. But for now, American tanks are advancing toward Bastogne.

◆　◆　◆

The smoke clears, and the tanks burst out of the forest and into an open field dotted with parachutes. First Lieutenant Charles Boggess opens the turret of Cobra King and lifts himself up through the hatch. Soldiers in uniform crouch in foxholes, their guns aimed his way. "Come here. Come on out," he shouts. He does not yell in German, hoping to find an American reply.

There is no answer. A tense moment passes. With his head and chest completely exposed to rifle fire, Lieutenant Boggess considers his options.

The Sherman 75mm barrel pivots until it is aimed directly at the foxholes. Private James G. Murphy has already loaded a round, and the gunner, Corporal Milton Dickerman, awaits the order to fire.

"Come on out," Boggess nervously shouts again.

A lone soldier walks forward.

"I'm Lieutenant Webster, of the 326th Engineers, 101st Airborne Division," he says. "Glad to see you."

Cobra King rolls into the heart of the town, followed by a convoy of Sherman tanks.

Bastogne has been relieved.

Patton's audacious plan has succeeded.

◆ ◆ ◆

The next morning—December 27, 1944—George Patton once again walks to the front of a small Catholic chapel and drops to his knees in prayer. He begins with an air of contrition.

> *Sir, this is Patton again, and I beg to report complete progress. Sir, it seems to me that You have been much better informed about the situation than I was, because it was that awful weather which I cursed so much which made it possible for the German army to commit suicide. That, Sir, was a brilliant military move, and I bow humbly to Your supreme genius.*

Patton writes home to his wife, Beatrice, "The relief of Bastogne is the most brilliant operation we have thus far performed, and is in my opinion the outstanding achievement of this war.

"Now the enemy must dance to our tune, not we to his."

CHAPTER 15

WASHINGTON, D.C.

JANUARY 20, 1945

IT IS AN UNPRECEDENTED FOURTH inaugural for Franklin Delano Roosevelt. War is not far from any American's mind even on this day.

Wounded soldiers—many on crutches—are among the eight thousand invited guests tromping through harsh weather to witness Franklin Delano Roosevelt's swearing-in as president of the United States. This will be the first inaugural address during wartime since Abraham Lincoln spoke eighty years ago in 1865. Also, this is the first inaugural to be held at the White House, in "the president's backyard," as the south lawn is known. Finally, this is the first and only time an American president will be sworn in for a fourth term.

Four thousand miles away, General George S. Patton is not paying attention to the inaugural. Patton thinks highly of

Roosevelt—and the president fondly calls him "old cavalryman" and "our greatest fighting general, a pure joy"—but Patton is busy directing the mop-up of the battlefields of Luxembourg and Belgium and dealing with military politics.

On February 10, Dwight Eisenhower will once again order Patton and his Third Army to stop their drive east and go on the defensive.

At the same time, Ike selects British Field Marshal Bernard Montgomery to lead the main Allied invasion force that will cross the strategically vital Rhine River. Stretching eight hundred miles down the length of Germany from the North Sea to Switzerland, the Rhine is the last great obstacle between the Allies and the German heartland. By selecting Montgomery over Patton, Eisenhower is almost assuring that the British commander will

General Eisenhower (second from left) in Bastogne with Generals Bradley and Patton. The man on the far left is Sergeant Jules Grad, an Army reporter.
[Mary Evans Picture Library]

know the glory of being the first of the Western Allies to reach Berlin.

It is as if Patton's monumental achievement at Bastogne never happened.

"It was rather amusing, though perhaps not flattering, to note that General Eisenhower never mentioned the Bastogne offensive," he writes of his most recent discussions with Eisenhower. Then, referring to the emergency meeting in Verdun that turned the tide of the Battle of the Bulge, he adds, "Although this was the first time I had seen him since the nineteenth of December—when he seemed much pleased to have me at the critical point."

At the end of the war, Field Marshal Montgomery (pointing at map) briefs his liaison officers at his headquarters in Germany, April 1945. [Mary Evans Picture Library]

Even more galling, not just to Patton but also to American soldiers, is that Montgomery has publicly taken credit for the Allied victory at the Battle of the Bulge. Monty insists that it is his British forces of the Twenty-First Army Group, not American GIs, who stopped the German advance.

"As soon as I saw what was happening," Montgomery stated at a January 7 press conference, "I took steps to ensure that the Germans would never get over the Meuse. I carried out certain movements to meet the threatened danger. I employed the whole power of the British group of armies."

Montgomery's stunning press conference comments did considerable damage to Anglo-American relations. To Patton, it seems outrageous that Montgomery should be rewarded for such deceptive behavior.

Yet that's precisely what Eisenhower does.

Although four American soldiers serve along the German front for every British one, Eisenhower has caved in to pressure from Winston Churchill in selecting Monty to lead the main charge across the Rhine. The reasons are political, but also practical: The crucial Ruhr industrial region is in northern Germany, as are Montgomery's troops. Theoretically, Monty is capable of quickly laying waste to the lifeblood of Germany's war machine.

Nevertheless, the decision makes George S. Patton furious.

CHAPTER 16

AUSCHWITZ-BIRKENAU

OŚWIĘCIM, POLAND ✠ JANUARY 26, 1945 ✠ 1 A.M.

THE SOVIET ARMY HAS BLOWN through the German defenses in Czechoslovakia and Hungary and is rapidly advancing west. The Soviets captured Warsaw and now race through Poland, intent on occupying Berlin before the Americans and the other Allies can get there. The Russians are so close to the concentration camp in Auschwitz that the boom of their artillery can be heard in the distance, and the occasional barrel flash of a launching shell lights the horizon. The Nazi guards at the camp who have been ordered to destroy the crematoriums are anxious to be away, afraid they will soon become Russian prisoners—a certain death sentence for them.

The earth convulses as the crematorium Krema V explodes. Tongues of flame turn the coal-black winter sky a bright red. The guards watch the inferno intently, but only for as long as it takes to know that the destruction is complete and that there will be no need for more dynamite charges. The grisly evidence is now destroyed.

Krema—that horrible redbrick building where hundreds of thousands of prisoners entered, but none walked out. Jews, Roma, homosexuals, and the handicapped were led inside, locked in an airtight room, and gassed with a cyanide-based pesticide known as Zyklon B dropped through the ventilation system. Death came slowly as the prisoners, unable to breathe, tried to claw their way out of the room, leaving grotesque scratch marks on the walls.

Now Krema V is no more. The other four Auschwitz crematoriums have also been detonated. Adolf Hitler has ordered that the murders be stopped and all physical proof of his atrocities destroyed.

Auschwitz in the distance.
[Mary Evans Picture Library]

From left to right, Anne Frank, Ellen Weinberger, Margot Frank, and Gabrielle Kahn have tea with their dolls after fleeing to Amsterdam from Germany.
[United States Holocaust Memorial Museum, courtesy of Penny Boyer]

Several thousand prisoners mill about the camp or huddle inside the barracks as the guards speed away into the night. The prisoners wait. Are they really free? Or will some worse fate befall them? Because if they've learned anything from their time in the death camps, it's that when things can't seem to get more horrific, they always do.

◆ ◆ ◆

A fifty-five-year-old German Jew lies in his wooden bunk in the men's sick barracks at Auschwitz. It is 3 P.M. on January 27, 1945.

Otto Frank and his family moved to the Netherlands when the rise of Nazism increased anti-Jewish sentiment in Germany. Then the Nazis invaded the Netherlands, and the country was taken over.

Two years later, on June 25, 1942, the *Daily Telegraph* in London ran a story with the headline "Germans Murder 700,000 Jews in Poland." The *Times* of London was soon reporting, "Massacre of Jews: Over 1,000,000 Dead Since the War Began," whereupon the *Guardian* noted that seven million Jews were now in German custody and that Eastern Europe was a "vast slaughterhouse of Jews."

In Amsterdam, Frank's family went into hiding soon after those news reports emerged. Life was squalid and claustrophobic in their secret apartment, but at least they were free. For two long years the Franks evaded detection by the Nazis. They were less than a month away from the Allies' arrival in the Netherlands when the end came.

On August 4, 1944, a secret informant, whose name has never become known, gave away the family's hiding place to the Gestapo.

The Franks were arrested, and within a month, Otto, his wife, Edith, and his teenage daughters, Margot and Annelies, arrived at Auschwitz.

As soon as they disembarked from their cattle cars, families were disassembled. Men and women were separated, their children taken from them. Otto Frank has not seen his wife and daughters since September.

As he lies in his bunk this cold January day five months later, Frank does not know whether his family is alive or dead. He does not know that the women he loves so much have also suffered the indignities he has: being stripped naked, having their heads shaved to check for lice, then standing in line to get a number tattooed on their left forearms. That number, they were soon told, was their new identity. They no longer had a name.

During their time in hiding, young Annelies—just Anne to her family—kept a detailed journal of what their life in hiding was like. She is five feet four inches tall, with an easy smile and dimples. Her eyes are gray, with just the slightest trace of green. Anne's wavy hair, before the Germans shaved her skull smooth, was brown and fell to her shoulders.

◆   ◆   ◆

Incredibly, both girls are still alive as Otto Frank hears ecstatic shouts from outside his barracks. "We're free," the prisoners are shouting. "We're free."

Soviet soldiers are marching into the camp, taking careful and cautious steps, suspicious of a surprise German attack. They wear winter-white camouflage uniforms and appear out of the snowy mist like apparitions.

The Soviet soldiers are not sure what they have stumbled upon. There are corpses everywhere, and people still alive but looking like skeletons, with the hollow faces of those close to death. "When I saw the people, it was skin and bones. They had no shoes, and it was freezing. They couldn't even turn their heads; they stood like dead people," one of the first Russian officers into the camp will later remember. "I told them, 'The Russian army liberates you!' They couldn't understand. Some few who could touched our arms and said, 'Is it true? Is it real?'"

The Soviet soldiers move from barrack to barrack, shocked at what they see. "When I opened the barrack, I saw blood, dead people, and in between them, women still alive and naked," Soviet officer Anatoly Shapiro will remember. "It stank;

Twelve-year-old Anne Frank models a new coat in a photograph taken in Amsterdam, 1941. [United States Holocaust Memorial Museum, courtesy of Eva Schloss]

you couldn't stay a second. No one took the dead to a grave. It was unbelievable. The soldiers from my battalion asked me, 'Let us go. We can't stay. This is unbelievable.'"

Despite all the horrors these soldiers have seen during their

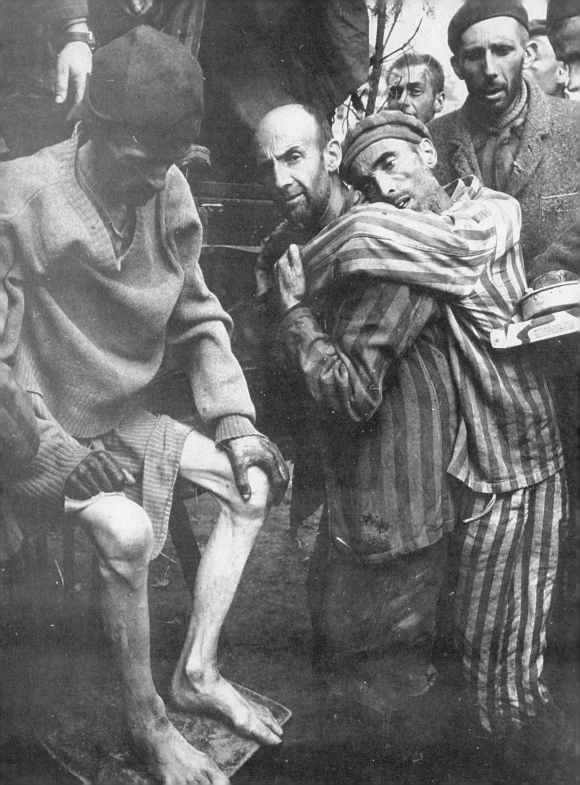

march to Germany, they know that Auschwitz is different. "We ran up to them," ten-year-old survivor Eva Mozes and her twin sister, Miriam, will later recall. "They gave us hugs, cookies, and chocolates. Being so alone, a hug meant more than anybody could imagine, because that replaced the human worth we were starving for. We were not only starved for worth, we were starved for human kindness, and the Soviet army did provide some of that."

◆　◆　◆

Otto Frank rises from his sickbed to celebrate his newfound freedom. His thoughts immediately turn to finding his family.

But he will never find them. Instead, in the weeks and months and years to come, he will discover threads of their travels, allowing him to piece together their horrible ends.

Otto Frank's beloved wife, Edith, died of starvation just six weeks ago right here at Auschwitz. His daughters were transferred to Bergen-Belsen in northern Germany in the fall of 1944. Margot Frank died of typhus in early 1945.

Her sister, Anne, is still alive when her father is liberated but has just weeks to live. She will die bald and covered with insect bites, her emaciated body finally done in by a typhoid outbreak that will kill seventeen thousand inmates at Bergen-Belsen.

She is just fifteen years old.

Survivors of the concentration camp at Wöbbelin, Germany, are evacuated to a U.S. field hospital for care. [United States Holocaust Memorial Museum, National Archives and Records Administration, College Park Time/Life Syndication, courtesy of Arnold Bauer Barach]

IN THE
FÜHRERBUNKER

CHAPTER 17

BERLIN, GERMANY

JANUARY 30, 1945

Adolf Hitler continues to blame the Jews for Germany's problems. It has been two decades since he spoke or had contact with a Jewish person, and yet he is obsessed with eradicating them from the planet.

On this, the twelfth anniversary of the day he became chancellor, he tells the German people, "Judaism began systematically to undermine our nation from within."

Hitler's physical health is declining. His hands shake. His eyes water. He is now getting twice-a-day injections of methamphetamine so he can function. This is not the trim, vibrant man whom Eva Braun first met. Fifteen years ago, in 1929, a man who was

A young member of the Hitler Youth hands Hitler a letter written by his mother. [United States Holocaust Memorial Museum, courtesy of Richard Freimark and William O. McWorkman]

Eva Braun, about age twenty.
[Mary Evans Picture Library]

introduced to her as "Mr. Wolf" came into the shop where she was working to speak with the owner. She was invited to have lunch with the group and remembered that he seemed to be "devouring me with his eyes." As most people were, she was attracted to his charisma and power. And he was kind to her. Even now, he and Eva Braun carry on the charade that the war can be won. But Hitler's location inside the bombed-out ruins of Berlin tells the true story. It has been two weeks since his personal train slunk into the once proud capital of Germany in the dead of night. The curtains were drawn as a precaution against Allied bombing—though that is really more of a habit than anything else. The Luftwaffe, the German air force, has been destroyed. American and British bombers are free to attack Berlin in broad daylight—which they do most days by nine in the morning, as the city's embattled residents hurry off to work—and again at night.

From left to right, Eva Braun, Hitler, Blondi, Sepp Dietrich, and Albert Speer. [Mary Evans Picture Library]

How different this is from twelve years earlier, when Hitler came to Berlin as the newly appointed second-in-command to Field Marshal Paul von Hindenburg, the president of Germany. Then Hitler and his Nazi Party were seen as the saviors of the country where six million people were unemployed. More than fifty thousand people are said to have joined the Nazi Party in the weeks following Hitler's rise to power. At that time he told the German people,

The National Government will regard it as its first and foremost duty to revive in the nation the spirit of unity and co-operation. It will preserve and defend those basic principles on which our nation has been built. It regards Christianity as the foundation of our national morality, and the family as the basis of national life.

Now he knows that his dream of the ideal Germany is in ruins. There will be no stopping the Allies on the western front. To the east, where the Russian superiority is eleven soldiers for every one German fighter, the situation is even worse.

On this very day—January 30, 1945—Hitler's minister of armaments, Albert Speer, has sent Hitler a memo informing the Führer that the war is lost. Germany does not have the industrial capacity necessary to churn out the tanks, planes, submarines, and bombs necessary to defeat the Allies. Nor does it have the manpower.

Paul von Hindenburg and Hitler, 1933. [Mary Evans Picture Library]

Nevertheless, Hitler has no plans to surrender. In his anniversary speech today, he says,

> On this day I do not want to leave any doubt about something else. Against an entire hostile world I once chose my road, according to my inner call, and strode it, as an unknown and nameless man, to final success; often they

reported I was dead and always they wished I were, but in the end I remained victor in spite of all. My life today is with an equal exclusiveness determined by the duties incumbent on me.

The Reich Chancellery in Berlin housed the Berlin parliament and Hitler's offices. [Mary Evans Picture Library]

Hitler now makes his home in central Berlin, underground, in an elaborate bunker built underneath the Reich Chancellery. The complex consists of two levels: The upper-level Vorbunker contains a conference room, dining facility, kitchen, water storage room, and bedrooms for support staff, which number more than two dozen. Below that is the Führerbunker, with lavishly decorated rooms for Hitler and Eva Braun. A large oil painting of his personal hero, Frederick the Great, covers one wall. The entire complex lies beneath a garden, where Hitler goes most days to walk Blondi.

Eva Braun still tends to him, though she does not live inside the bunker with him. She remains calm, believing that Hitler's cruel genius can win the day. Living in an underground bunker is just one more precaution that is necessary in a time of war. Adding to the air of normalcy is that Blondi has new puppies, which make their home in the bunker as well.

Even though he fears that a direct hit from an Allied bomb will kill him instantly, Adolf Hitler believes he will be saved. In the conclusion to his speech, he says,

> *However grave the crisis may be at the moment, it will, despite everything, finally be mastered by our unalterable will, by our readiness for sacrifice and by our abilities. We shall overcome this calamity, too, and this fight, too, will not be won by central Asia [meaning Russia] but by Europe; and at its head will be the nation that has*

represented Europe against the East for fifteen hundred years and shall represent it for all times: our Greater German Reich, the German nation.

Adolf Hitler has ninety days to live. He will never leave Berlin again.

CHAPTER 18

REMAGEN, GERMANY

MARCH 7, 1945

O N MARCH 7, A SMALL AMERICAN unit of armored infantry succeeded in crossing the Rhine in the town of Remagen, sixty-three miles north of Patton's location in Trier. The incredulous Americans could not believe that the bridge remained intact, and crossed immediately. And while they were not able to advance beyond a small toehold on the Rhine's eastern shore, the symbolism of the Allied achievement struck such fear in the minds of the Nazi high command that Adolf Hitler ordered the execution by firing squad of the four officers he considered responsible for not destroying the bridge. The men were forced to kneel, then shot in

[pages 148–149] *Troops of the U.S. 9th Armored Division head for the Ludendorff Bridge at Remagen, Germany. They were some of the first soldiers to cross the Rhine River.* [Mary Evans Picture Library]

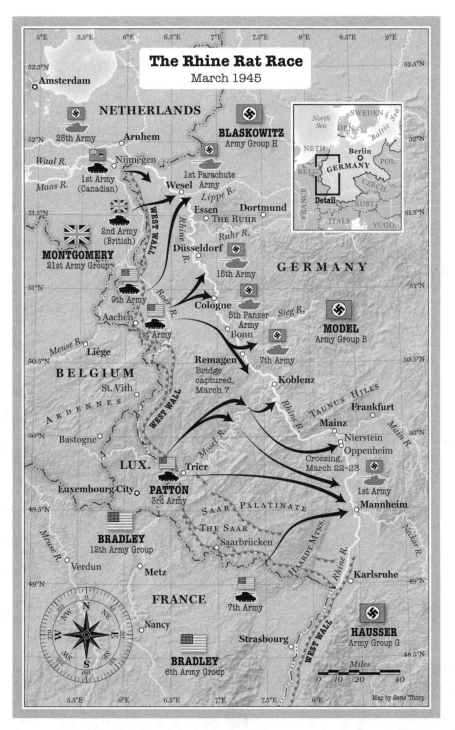

The Rhine Rat Race
March 1945

Amsterdam

NETHERLANDS

25th Army

Arnhem

Nijmegen

BLASKOWITZ
Army Group H

1st Army
(Canadian)

Waal R.

Maas R.

Wesel

1st Parachute
Army

Lippe R.

Essen

Dortmund

THE RUHR

2nd Army
(British)

WEST WALL

MONTGOMERY
21st Army Group

Düsseldorf

Ruhr R.

Rhine R.

GERMANY

9th Army

Aachen

Roer R.

15th Army

Cologne

Bonn

5th Panzer
Army

Sieg R.

MODEL
Army Group B

1st Army

Meuse R.

Liège

BELGIUM

St. Vith

A R D E N N E S

Bastogne

WEST WALL

Remagen
Bridge
captured,
March 7

7th Army

Koblenz

Rhine R.

T A U N U S   H I L L S

Frankfurt

Mainz

Main R.

LUX.

Trier

Mosel R.

Nierstein
Oppenheim

Crossing,
March 22–23

Luxembourg City

PATTON
3rd Army

1st Army

Mannheim

BRADLEY
12th Army Group

S A A R   P A L A T I N A T E

THE SAAR

Saarbrücken

HAARDT MTS.

Rhine R.

Neckar R.

Verdun

Metz

Meuse R.

FRANCE

7th Army

Nancy

Karlsruhe

Strasbourg

WEST WALL

HAUSSER
Army Group G

BRADLEY
6th Army Group

Miles
0 10 20 40

Map by Gene Thorp

North
Sea

SWEDEN

DEN.

Baltic Sea

NETH

Berlin

POL.

BELG.

GERMANY

FRANCE

CZECH.

Detail

AUST.

ITALY

YUGO.

N
NW   NE
W   E
SW   SE
S

Map legend is on page viii.

the back of the neck. The final letters they had written to family were burned.

Hitler then ordered the great commando Otto Skorzeny to assemble a team of swimmers to float down the Rhine and attach explosives to the Remagen Bridge. The mission failed when all of Skorzeny's amphibious commandos were discovered by sharp-eyed American sentries along the shore and were either killed or captured.

So the Allies still hold the bridge but are unable to advance farther without the assistance of a greater fighting force.

CHAPTER 19

TRIER, GERMANY

MARCH 13, 1945 ✠ MORNING

GEORGE S. PATTON UNDERSTANDS THE SIGNIFICANCE of Remagen. "Ninth Armored Division of the Third Corps," he wrote in his journal on March 7, "got a bridge intact over the Rhine at Remagen. This may have a fine influence on our future movements. I hope we get one also."

But even if he can't find an intact bridge, Patton is determined to beat Montgomery across the Rhine.

Patton has just ten days.

Now he is on the move. Finally.

Sergeant John Mims drives Patton in his open-air jeep, with its three-star flags over the wheel wells. The snows of the cruel sub-zero winter are finally melting. Patton and Mims pass frozen, legs-up carcasses of dead cattle as the road winds from Luxembourg into Germany. Hulks of destroyed Sherman M4s litter the countryside—so many tanks, in fact, that Patton makes a mental note to investigate which type of enemy round defeated each of them. This is Patton's way of helping the U.S. Army build better armor for fighting the next war.

Third Army is advancing into Germany. Patton has sensed a weakness in the German lines and is eager to press his advantage.

He has convinced Eisenhower to let him attack two hundred miles to the south. The plan to invade southern Germany's Palatinate region, an area west of the Rhine, came to Patton in a dream. It was fully formed, down to the last logistical detail. "Whether ideas like this are inspiration or insomnia, I don't know," he writes in his journal. "I do things by sixth sense." Patton's plan to invade the Palatinate is approved by Eisenhower. However, Patton is not given permission to cross the Rhine should the opportunity arise.

Then again, following the old adage that it is easier to seek forgiveness than to ask permission, Patton doesn't plan on asking for permission to ford the mighty river.

◆　◆　◆

Patton's military ambitions for the assault are many, among them the devastation of all German forces guarding the heavily fortified Siegfried Line, a four-hundred-mile defensive array of eighteen thousand bunkers and interlocking rows of pyramid-shaped concrete antitank obstacles nicknamed "dragon's teeth." Hitler built the barrier between 1936 and 1938, anticipating by almost a decade the day that some great army—in this case, that of the Allies—would attempt to invade the Fatherland.

Privately, however, Patton admits that not all his goals are tactical. The war is now personal. The man who lives for battle wants to be judged by his actions, not his words. The war will end soon. Patton would love nothing more than for the spotlight to shine on his amazing generalship at least one more time.

So it is that the Third Army romps through the Palatinate on what Colonel Abe Abrams of the Fourth Armored Division calls the Rhine Rat Race. It travels with ample supplies of metal decking and pontoons. Patton hopes to build temporary bridges across the Rhine, well ahead of Montgomery and his Twenty-First Army Group.

◆ ◆ ◆

As the days tick down to Montgomery's Operation Plunder, Patton's army overwhelms the German army in southern Germany, capturing sixty-eight thousand prisoners and three thousand square miles of German countryside. The Siegfried Line proves no match for the Third Army. Patton's forces seem to be everywhere. Even the hilliest terrain sports hundreds of U.S. tanks and infantry units rolling down roads long considered "impassable to armor."

"The enemy," notes one American soldier, is "a beaten mass of men, women, and children, interspersed with diehard Nazis."

Patton writes candidly to Beatrice about the condition of the German people. "I saw one woman with a perambulator full of her

[next pages] *Hitler admires a model of the Siegfried Line while staffers look on, 1939.* [Bridgeman Art Library]

worldly goods sitting by it on a hill, crying. An old man with a wheelbarrow and three little children wringing his hands. A woman with five children and a tin cup crying. In hundreds of villages there is not a living thing, not even a chicken. Most of the houses are heaps and stones. They brought it on themselves, but these poor peasants are not responsible.

"I am getting soft?" Patton asks Beatrice rhetorically.

◆　◆　◆

Montgomery is still waiting. The British commander is assembling the largest amphibious operation since D-day. His staff checks and rechecks every detail, from the perceived numerical superiority of Allied forces to the number of assault boats required to cross the Rhine, to even the tonnage of munitions that British bombers will drop to root out any concealed German resistance.

Meanwhile, Patton attacks. His Palatinate campaign will go down in history as one of

Advancing American troops pass captured German soldiers (center) near Giessen, Germany, in 1945.
[Mary Evans Picture Library]

YOU ARE NOW
CROSSING THE
RHINE RIVER
THROUGH COURTESY
OF E CO. 17 ARMD
ENGR BN AND
C CO 202
ENGR. C. BN

the great strategies of the war. Even the Germans will say so. And their praise for Patton will be their biggest show of respect. "The greatest threat," captured German Lieutenant Colonel Konrad Freiherr von Wangenheim reveals during his interrogation, "was the whereabouts of the feared U.S. Army. General Patton is always the topic of military discussion. Where is he? When will he attack? Where? How? With what?"

Von Wangenheim goes on to add: "General Patton is the most feared general on all fronts.... The tactics of General Patton are daring and unpredictable.... He is the most modern general

U.S. troops cross a pontoon bridge over the Rhine River. The soldiers in the engineer divisions who built the bridge left a sign.
[Mary Evans Picture Library]

and the best commander of armored and infantry troops combined."

Patton's tanks are riding roughshod over the rugged countryside. Patton was nothing short of brilliant at Bastogne, and now he is the same in the Palatinate.

"We are the eighth wonder of the world," Patton says of the Third Army on March 19, congratulating himself on yet another success. "And I had to beg, lie, and steal to get started."

Patton's forces capture the pivotal city of Koblenz, at the meeting of the Rhine and Moselle Rivers. He now has eight full divisions lined up along the western shore of the Rhine, the tank barrels aimed directly at the eastern bank.

Now all Patton needs to do is find a place to cross.

◆   ◆   ◆

The date is March 22, 1945. Two hours before midnight, under cover of darkness, a Third Army patrol paddles across the Rhine at Nierstein in flimsy canvas assault boats. The slap of their paddles stroking the swift waters goes unheard. They report back that no enemy troops are in the vicinity. When Patton receives the news, he immediately orders that bridging material be sent forward. By late afternoon March 23, hastily built pontoon bridges span the river. Consisting of several floating barrels topped with steel tread, these bridges can be built in hours. They are highly effective in moving men and material across a river—but also highly unstable. Despite that, an entire division of Patton's army is soon across.

Patton calls General Bradley, but instead of making the sort of bold pronouncement that would inform the Germans of his precise location, he sets aside his pride in a moment of caution.

"Don't tell anyone, but I'm across," Patton informs Bradley.

"Well, I'll be damned," Bradley responds. "You mean across the Rhine?"

"Sure I am. Sneaked a division over last night. But there are so few Krauts around here they don't know it yet. So don't make any announcement. We'll keep it a secret until we see how it goes."

It goes well—but only for a short time.

The sight of thousands of men marching across temporary pontoon bridges is hard to conceal. The German air force discovers Third Army's encroachment at dawn. Disregarding Allied air superiority, Luftwaffe fighters patrol low above the Rhine, searching for signs of soldiers, vehicles, and supplies that betray the Allied buildup. The pilots radio back what they see, then strafe the intruders with rounds of machine gun and cannon fire.

But the German pilots are *too* bold, and in their determination to throw back Patton's invaders, thirty-three Luftwaffe planes are blasted out of the sky by precision firing from Third Army's anti-aircraft guns. The German pilots are so low that bailing out and parachuting to safety is not an option. The American soldiers continue their march across the swift blue waters of the Rhine, cheered throughout the day by the sight of enemy planes exploding all across the horizon and falling into the river with mighty splashes.

It is clear that the Americans no longer need to proceed under radio silence.

George S. Patton and his Third Army are now across the Rhine and prepared to invade the German heartland. Patton will take great pride in boasting of this accomplishment, at great expense to the British: "Without benefit of aerial bombardment, ground smoke, artillery preparation, and airborne assistance, the Third Army at 2200 hours, Thursday, 22 March 1945, crossed the Rhine River."

Montgomery's Twenty-First Army Group crossed the Rhine the evening of March 23, 1945. To be ready for this earth-shaking event, Churchill wrote a speech congratulating Field Marshal Montgomery for the first "assault" crossing over the Rhine River in modern history. The speech was recorded and, through some error by the British Broadcasting Corporation, was broadcast. The Third Army had been across the Rhine River for some twenty-four hours.

On March 31, 1945, Field Marshal Bernard Montgomery (in the beret) and Prime Minister Winston Churchill (second from right) cross the Rhine with American troops to observe the Allied advance into Germany. [Mary Evans Picture Library]

The bombed-out Chancellery, May 1, 1945.
[United States Holocaust Memorial Museum, courtesy
of the family of Raymond N. Born]

CHAPTER 20

BERLIN, GERMANY

APRIL 10, 1945 ✠ NIGHT

NOBODY STANDS AS ADOLF HITLER enters the conference room.

The Führer's entire body quivers as he assumes his usual place before the war map table. Hitler's hands shake, his head nods uncontrollably, and he is bent at the waist, too weak to stand upright. The distant thunder of Allied bombing shakes the concrete walls. Yet the Führer's eyes shine brightly behind his rimless pale green eyeglasses, showing no fear whatsoever as he gazes down at the current location of his armies. Most of what he sees, however, is not real; he is too deluded to know the truth. In his desperation to end the war on his terms, Hitler imagines nonexistent "ghost" divisions as he scrutinizes the map, and pictures thousands of tanks in places where there are none at all.

Meanwhile, private conversation hums as if the Führer had never even entered the upper-level room. German officers and Hitler's secretaries gossip and chitchat as if the most feared man in the world were not in their presence.

An Allied bomb explodes nearby. The room shudders. Lights sway, flickering temporarily, then return to full strength. All talk ceases. The military officers know better than to appear afraid, while the secretaries train their eyes on Hitler, waiting for his response.

"That was close!" Hitler says to no one in particular.

Weak smiles fill the room. Just weeks ago such informality would have been an unforgivable lapse in protocol, but living underground is taking its toll on Hitler's staff. They live in a world where the walls are made of hard rock, like a cave-dwelling prehistoric Germanic tribe. The cement corridors are narrow, painted the color of rust, and the ceilings are low. Rooms are all painted a dull gray, and the walls weep as moisture seeps through the rock. The residents have their own water supply from a deep artesian well. The energy for the switchboard, lights, and heat comes from a sixty-kilowatt diesel generator. The air comes from up above, but through a filter to ensure its purity.

The bunker is hardly pleasant. There are three separate security checkpoints just to get in, and all entrances are manned by guards carrying machine pistols and grenades. In this way, Hitler's headquarters is, in fact, a prison.

"The whole atmosphere down there was debilitating," one German soldier who served in the bunker will later remember. "In the long hours of the night it could be deathly silent, except for the hum of the generator. . . . Then there was the fetid odor of boots, sweaty woolen uniforms, strong-smelling cleaning disinfectants. At times toward the end, when the drainage backed up, it was as pleasant as working in a public urinal."

The bunker's residents must endure the claustrophobia of rarely going up to the garden to feel the sun on their faces. The group has become so used to the sight of their Führer that even the lowest level staffers no longer feel the need to cut short their conversations when Hitler is in their presence.

Yet the informality belies the truth: Everyone—with the exception of Adolf Hitler—is terrified. "You felt it to the point of physical illness," one German officer will later write. "Nothing was authentic except fear."

And yet Adolf Hitler is convinced that the war can still be won.

Aboveground, the Allies are bombing around the clock—the United States Army Air Forces in the daylight and the British Royal Air Force by night. Berlin is a city in ruins. Of its 1,562,000 homes and apartments, one third have been completely destroyed. Almost fifty thousand citizens have died, more than twice the number who died as a result of the German bombings of London. Those still alive sleep most nights in subways and cellars. Despite the chaos, there is an amazing sense of routine to life on the streets of Berlin: Mail is delivered each day; the Berlin Philharmonic performs concerts at night; the subway runs on time; bakeries open their doors each morning.

One quiet reality, however, pervades life in Berlin: The Russian

army is less than forty miles away. Refugees pouring into the capital from the east, seeking to escape the brutal oppressors, tell horror stories of murder and rape. And while some wealthy Berliners are secretly making plans to flee the city and perhaps find sanctuary in Switzerland, most citizens are stuck. They cannot run. The Russians are to the east, and the Americans, British, Canadians, and French are to the west. So they remain, enduring the bombings, going about their business as best they can.

◆　◆　◆

Last month Hitler was visited by Joachim Peiper and Otto Skorzeny. His two favorite soldiers are soon to fight no more. In Vienna, Austria, Peiper and his

Hitler (right) and his personal adjunct, SS Group Leader Julius Schaub, visit the destroyed Chancellery in April 1945.
[Mary Evans Picture Library]

First SS Panzer Division have been defeated and disgraced in a last-ditch attempt to stop the Russian advance. Furious, Hitler has ordered Peiper and his men to remove the armbands bearing his name from their uniforms. Shortly after that, Peiper flees west and is captured by the Americans.

Skorzeny, a native of Vienna, hears that the Russians are about to enter that city and races there on April 10 with a team of commandos. He finds Vienna in flames. Instantly recognizing that the city will fall by morning, he and his commandos retreat. Their war is over. Skorzeny orders his men to hide themselves, while he escapes into the mountains, where he vacillates between suicide and fleeing Germany while he can still get out alive. In time, he chooses a third option—he surrenders to the Allies.

◆　◆　◆

In the pale artificial light of the bunker, Adolf Hitler continues to stare, hour after hour, at his map table; he waits for some sign that all will be well. He is determined that the war end on his own terms. "Think of Leonidas and his three hundred Spartans," he tells his personal secretary, referring to the ancient Greek warrior king of Sparta. "It does not suit us to let ourselves be slaughtered like sheep. They may exterminate us, but they will not be able to lead us to the slaughter."

Thus the Führer has begun a scorched-earth policy designed to deprive Germany's approaching conquerors of any form of sustenance. On March 19 he wrote a directive that orders: "All military, transportation, communications, industrial, and food supply facilities,

*Otto Skorzeny in November 1943. He fought fifteen saber duels as a young man.
In one, he received a deep cut on his cheek, which left him with a scar.*
[Mary Evans Picture Library]

as well as all other resources within the Reich which the enemy might use either immediately or in the foreseeable future for continuing the war, are to be destroyed."

This is all Hitler can do: prepare for the end. His attempt to cleanse mankind of perceived racial imperfections is over. As will soon be his life.

So as Hitler passes the time in the bunker, sleeping most days and staying up until dawn most nights to scrutinize plans for battles that will never be fought, he finds a most unusual way to maintain his optimism.

His source of hope is the soothing voice of his propaganda minister, Joseph Goebbels. Palsied tremors make it impossible for Hitler to turn the pages of a book, so he commands Goebbels to read aloud to him from Thomas Carlyle's biography of Frederick the Great; the eighteenth-century Prussian warrior king has always been an inspiration to the Führer.

Hitler specifically chooses the biography by Carlyle because he set forth the great man theory of history, which states, "The history of the world is but the biography of great men."

Leonidas was a great man.

Frederick was a great man.

Hitler considers himself a great man.

Early in the war, Hitler confers with his propaganda minister, Joseph Goebbels. [Mary Evans Picture Library]

Reclining on the bed in his personal quarters as Goebbels sits in a nearby chair, Hitler is calmed by words that make a vivid comparison between Frederick and his own current situation. It is a passage describing the winter of 1761–62, when all seemed lost during the Seven Years' War. Frederick had few allies at the time and was facing a multinational force that threatened to annihilate his Prussian troops. Hitler is also facing the end. Russian troops are poised to enter his capital city. So he finds solace in the lessons learned by this great man whom he reveres deeply.

◆　　◆　　◆

Just days later, Adolf Hitler receives another sign that Germany could still win the war. He summons all his top generals and ministers to the bunker to show them the news. "Here, you never wanted to believe it," he crows, distributing the report that he has just received.

The bunker erupts in cheers.

The news could not be more shocking: Hitler has outlived one of his biggest opponents.

American President Franklin Delano Roosevelt is dead.

At the Yalta Conference, in February 1945, allies (front row, left to right) Joseph Stalin, Franklin Roosevelt, and Winston Churchill meet to discuss the governance of post–World War II Axis countries.
[Mary Evans Picture Library]

CHAPTER 21

BAD HERSFELD, GERMANY

APRIL 12, 1945

EORGE PATTON IS JUST FINISHING his daily journal entries. The hour is late, but today has been extraordinary, and he needs to put every last detail on paper before going to bed. Finally, he closes his journal and puts down his pen.

Patton notices that his wristwatch needs winding. So he turns on the radio in the small truck trailer that serves as his field bedroom. He hopes to get the exact time from the British Broadcasting Corporation's evening broadcast. Instead, he hears the shocking news that FDR is no more.

This is the wretched conclusion to what has been the most nerve-wracking day Patton has endured thus far in the war. Just

Generals Bradley, Patton (behind Eisenhower), and Eisenhower inspect paintings stolen by the Nazis and stored in a salt mine in Merkers, Germany, April 12, 1945. [Alamy]

after breakfast, he met with Generals Dwight Eisenhower and Omar Bradley at his headquarters in an old Wehrmacht fort in Bad Hersfeld, one hundred miles east of the Rhine. Together they traveled to the town of Merkers, where Patton's army had made an incredible find.

The three men entered the mouth of a massive cave, where they boarded a flimsy wooden elevator that lowered them two thousand feet into a salt mine. The shaft was pitch-black, so once the daylight above them narrowed to a pinprick during the descent, Patton could not see the other occupants of the car. Noting that the elevator was suspended from a single thin cable, Patton couldn't help but quip about their plight. "If that clothesline should break," he joked grimly, "promotions in the United States Army would be considerably stimulated."

"George, that's enough," shot back a nervous Eisenhower. "No more cracks until we are above ground again."

The purpose of their descent is of worldwide significance. Troopers in Patton's Third Army accidentally discovered the Merkers mine while interrogating local citizens. The bombing of Berlin had forced the Nazis to smuggle their financial reserves out of the official bank in Berlin to a place of safety. They chose this remote salt mine. Literally hundreds of millions of dollars in the form of gold bars, currency, and priceless works of art were stored underground two hundred miles

A soldier of the Third U.S. Army holds a painting by the famous Spanish artist Goya that the Nazis had hidden in a wooden crate at the Merkers mine. [Alamy]

from Berlin. As Patton, Eisenhower, and Bradley stepped out of the darkness of the elevator into the brightly lit cave, the scene was surreal. Bags of gold and cash stretched as far as the eye could see. Hundreds of paintings and sculptures, one a bust of Egyptian Queen Nefertiti, lined the walls, along with world-famous paintings by Titian and Manet. That the wealth is now in the Allies' possession signifies the dissolution of the Nazi government. Without money, it can no longer wage war.

"In addition to the German Reichsmarks [currency] and gold bricks, there was a great deal of French, American, and British gold currency. Also, a number of suitcases filled with jewelry, such as silver and gold cigarette cases, wristwatch cases, spoons, forks, vases, gold-filled teeth, false teeth, etc.," Patton wrote in his journal. The majority of the currency had been looted from the various nations conquered by Nazi Germany; the jewelry and gold

General Eisenhower examines a suitcase full of silver items stolen from prisoners and stored at the Merkers mine. [Alamy]

and silver items were taken from prisoners at concentration camps; and the art from fourteen German museums.

◆ ◆ ◆

Later in the day, George Patton's mood abruptly shifted. The three generals lunched together, then toured the newly liberated concentration camp at Buchenwald, twenty-six miles east of the Merkers mine. It was Patton's Fourth Armored Division—the first tanks into Bastogne and the first to reach the Rhine—that had discovered Ohrdruf, a subcamp of Buchenwald. Unlike Auschwitz, where guards were so rattled by the approaching Russians that they fled before executing the inmates, the SS here had tried to kill the remaining prisoners. Most were shot. Many were so emaciated and malnourished that the bullet wounds in their skulls did not even bleed.

The work camp tour was horrendous. Each of the generals had seen death in many forms during their time in the military. They had seen men blown to pieces and others lose their faces to exploding shells. But nothing they had ever witnessed prepared them for Ohrdruf. "It was the most appalling sight imaginable," Patton will write in his journal.

"The smell of death overwhelmed us," Bradley wrote in his memoirs. "More than 3,200 naked, emaciated bodies had been thrown into shallow graves. Others lay in the street where they had fallen. Lice crawled over the yellowed skin of their sharp, bony frames." The generals saw the gallows, where men were hanged for

Four survivors of the Buchenwald concentration camp.
[United States Holocaust Memorial Museum, courtesy of David Cohen]

trying to escape, and the whipping tables, where beatings were administered at random.

At one point, Patton excused himself from the tour, then walked off to vomit at the side of a building. Ike's face "whitened into a mask" at the horror, Bradley wrote. "I was too revolted to speak."

Now, the news of Roosevelt's death and Harry Truman's ascendency to the office of president brings this day to a close.

[right] *A survivor of the Buchenwald concentration camp shows his arm tattooed with his identification number.* [United States Holocaust Memorial Museum, courtesy of Stanley Moroknek Wilton Gottlieb]

[below] *A former prisoner stands near a gallows at Buchenwald.* [United States Holocaust Memorial Museum, courtesy of Frank W. Towers]

A banner tied to a bombed-out building in Berlin reads, "We salute the first worker of Germany: Adolf Hitler." It was put up to celebrate Hitler's birthday in 1944.

[Mary Evans Picture Library]

CHAPTER 22

BERLIN, GERMANY

APRIL 20, 1945 ✠ MIDNIGHT

T HE MAN WHO WILL BE dead in ten days is marking his fifty-sixth birthday.

Adolf Hitler's mistress, Eva Braun, is in the mood to dance, but the Führer merely slumps on the blue-and-white couch in his underground bunker's sitting room. He stares into space, paying no attention to the playful Eva or to the sleek blue dress she is wearing. Even though she knows that Hitler doesn't like her to dress provocatively, on this occasion Eva does as she pleases.

The two of them, along with three of Hitler's female secretaries, sip champagne. It is the end of another long and depressing day for the Führer.

Adolf Hitler once dreamed of establishing Berlin as the world's most cosmopolitan city, despite its citizens having long considered him to be an unsophisticated bore. Back in the days when

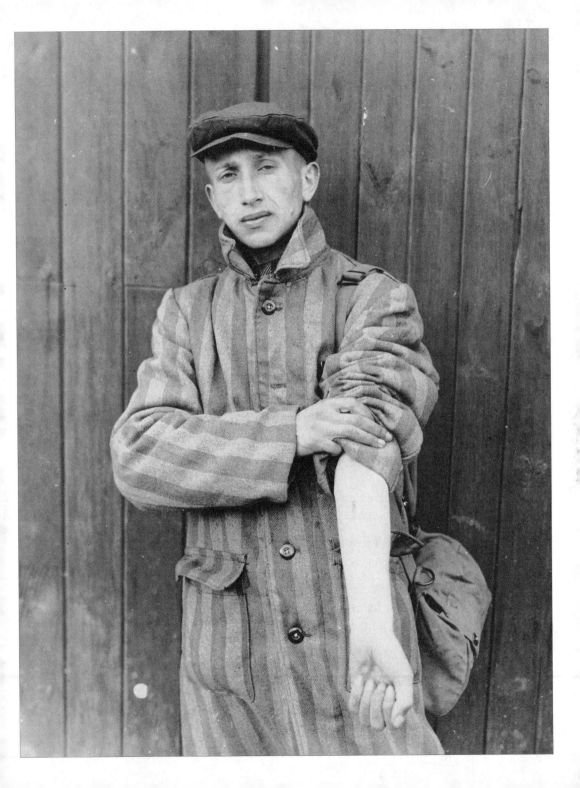

Germany held free elections, only 23 percent of the people of Berlin supported Hitler and his National Socialist German Workers' Party. Even now, thirteen years later, Berlin is considered the least Nazi of all cities in Germany. So Hitler planned to spite Berliners during the grand postwar rebuilding by renaming the city Germania, thus wiping Berlin off the map forever.

The advancing Russians know nothing about Germania. And they are also not waiting until the end of the war to wipe Berlin off the map.

Moving quickly, the armies of Joseph Stalin, premier of the Soviet Union, have the city almost completely surrounded. It is just a matter of time before it falls.

Only Hitler's most faithful followers remain in the bunker. Many of the elite officers are running for their lives, desperately hoping to get out of Berlin, hoping to adopt anonymous new identities. Martin Bormann, head of the Nazi Party Chancellery, continues to prove his loyalty by remaining in the bunker. Hitler is glad. It has been said that Bormann is so threatening he can "slit a throat with a whisper." A testimony to his character comes from none other than Hitler, the most callous of men. The Führer deems Bormann to be utterly "ruthless"—and thinks him indispensable.

Bormann is now upstairs on the top floor of the bunker, hard at work despite the late hour and the approaching danger.

Russian soldiers pose near the Reichstag in Berlin on May 1, 1945. Six days later, Germany will formally surrender. [Mary Evans Picture Library]

There is still time for Hitler to find a way out of Berlin. The Soviets are closing in, but some roads remain open. As recently as yesterday, the Führer was planning to escape to his Eagle's Nest retreat, high in southern Germany's mountains. Hitler even sent some members of the household staff ahead to prepare for his arrival. But he has since changed his mind, deciding to stay in the bunker, hoping against hope that the phantom divisions seen only by him will somehow repel the Russians.

Quietly, Hitler announces he is going to bed. He looks awful as he stands to walk the five steps into his bedroom—face pale, back stooped, eyes bloodshot from fatigue, his entire body shaking. He is beyond medical help. Hitler had his cocaine eyedrops administered to him this morning, but tomorrow he is sending Dr. Morell ahead to the Eagle's Nest, explaining that "drugs can't help me anymore."

With those words, Hitler admits defeat. There will be no Germania, just as there will no longer be a Nazi Germany—or an Adolf Hitler. The Führer can hear Russian artillery shelling Berlin, the explosions resounding through the city, thundering closer and closer to the Tiergarten, the Reichstag, and then, inevitably, shaking the ground directly above him in the Reich Chancellery Park. Hitler does not know if the bunker's thick roof can handle a direct hit, but he likes his chances inside his underground fortress better

Martin Bormann (left) and Rudolf Hess leave a meeting in 1935. Hess was Hitler's deputy führer. [Mary Evans Picture Library]

than on top, out in the open. Earlier today, Hitler walked up the steps into the garden and spoke to a group of young boys from the Hitler Youth who had distinguished themselves in the face of Russian tanks. With the rumble of artillery as a backdrop, Hitler reviewed the rows of assembled young soldiers, his frail body all but swallowed up inside his brownish-green overcoat. Despite his obvious palsy, he shook each and every young man's hand. Then, the Führer's mind clearly elsewhere, he exhorted them to save Berlin. "*Heil Euch*," he barked as words of praise before descending once again into the bunker— "Hail to you."

That ceremony marked the last time Adolf Hitler would ever see the light of day.

That was hours ago. Now, Eva Braun helps Hitler to bed, assisting him as he changes out of his uniform and into his plain white nightshirt. Thanks to years of living nocturnally, his body is "bright white," in the words of one secretary.

Eva does not get in bed with her beloved Adolf.

On April 20, 1945, his fifty-sixth birthday, Hitler left his bunker to greet members of the Hitler Youth. This is the last known photograph of Hitler alive. [Mary Evans Picture Library]

Instead, she steps back into the sitting room, closing the door dividing the two rooms behind her.

Now that the Führer is asleep, it's time to party.

"Eva Braun wanted to numb the fear that had awoken in her heart," Traudl Junge, one of the secretaries sipping champagne in Hitler's sitting room, will one day remember. "She wanted to celebrate once again, to dance, to drink, to forget."

Eva beckons the three young women to follow. The group climbs the steps to the second floor. They sweep through the bunker, rounding up everyone, even serious Martin Bormann.

The party marches through the secret underground tunnel connecting the bunker with the Reich Chancellery, where Hitler keeps a small apartment. The paintings have been removed and the furniture has been transferred down into the bunker, but there is still a record player in the room—and one very special record: "Blood Red Roses Speak of Happiness to You."

Eva Braun knows the words by heart. She and Adolf Hitler have listened to this record by the Max Mensing Orchestra over and over again. The Führer enjoys classical music—and even the solos of Jewish pianist Artur Schnabel—but the dance orchestra sound of "Blood Red Roses" is *their* song.

Champagne bottles are uncorked. The music is turned up loud. Eva Braun, so desperate to dance, whirls around the room, alone

A Berlin street fills with smoke after an American bombing raid in February 1945. [Mary Evans Picture Library]

Johanna Wolf (left), one of Hitler's former secretaries, and Ingeborg Sperr, Rudolf Hess's former secretary, wait to testify at the International Military Tribunal in Nuremberg, Germany. [National Archives and Records Administration, College Park]

and with anyone else who will dance with her. Blond and vivacious, she is the life of the party.

A distant explosion makes the room shake. The party ceases, but only temporarily. So Eva Braun dances on, "in a desperate frenzy, like a woman who has already felt the faint breath of death," Traudl Junge will remember. Her thirty-three-year-old friend has just ten days before she will bite into a cyanide capsule and take her own life.

"No one said anything about the war. No one mentioned victory. No one mentioned death. This was a party given by ghosts."

This photograph of Eva Braun was found among her possessions after her death. Date unknown. [Mary Evans Picture Library]

CHAPTER 23

WALDENBURG, GERMANY

APRIL 15, 1945

PATTON IS IN A PENSIVE mood. His Third Army is waiting in place. It is still a powerful force. In fact, Patton has just been given an additional three tank divisions. The Third Army was poised to wheel north to capture Berlin—as it had made a hard left turn and liberated Bastogne—but Eisenhower refused to grant permission. The Allied supreme commander has been communicating directly with the Russian generals now approaching the German capital. Ike has promised them that they can have Hitler all to themselves. So Patton and Lieutenant General Jacob Devers's armies will carry out the final American attacks of the war in southern Germany and leave Berlin to the Russians.

British forces under Field Marshal Montgomery are also ordered away from Berlin to secure the Danish border.

As the Russians pound the Nazi capital city with artillery, the

Although they were not allowed to advance into Berlin, soldiers of Patton's 12th Armored Division continued to find Nazis in the surrounding forests.

[Department of Defense Visual Information]

German people steel themselves for the inevitable moment when those they consider "subhumans" take over. Throughout Germany, fear of the Russians is everywhere. During the next month, millions of civilian refugees will flee toward the American lines—only to be turned back. More than a million German soldiers have already raised their hands in surrender and will not have to face the Russians. In fact, so many German fighters are giving up that the Allies no longer accept all prisoners of war because it is impossible to house and feed so many men. Thus, a number of terrified Germans are turned back to fend for themselves against the rampaging Russians. In early May, when the men of the once feared Eleventh Panzer Division attempt to quit the war, the Third Army will accept them as prisoners only under the condition that they bring their own food.

As Patton sips coffee in his headquarters, he knows that his future may lie as a civilian. He has once again appeared on the cover of *Time* magazine and is finally getting the public respect and glory he so desperately craves.

But the war is still ongoing. There are four million Allied soldiers in Germany right now, and three million of them are American.

CHAPTER 24

WIESENBURG FOREST

THIRTY MILES WEST OF BERLIN ✠ APRIL 23, 1945 ✠ 12:45 A.M.

G ENERAL WALTHER WENCK, COMMANDER OF the German Twelfth Army with the mission to guard against an Allied attack from the west, is up past midnight in his headquarters. It is a gamekeeper's house hidden in a thick forest thirty miles west of Berlin. The location is an ideal hiding place from Allied reconnaissance planes.

The phone rings. Wenck answers, only to learn that he will soon be paid a visit by Field Marshal Wilhelm Keitel, Adolf Hitler's arrogant commander of the armed forces—and a man whom Wenck loathes.

Walther Wenck is a fine officer. At forty-four, he is the youngest general in the German armed forces and bears the nickname Boy General. Currently, Wenck has taken it upon himself to house and feed a half million war refugees who have fled Berlin. He does

this without informing his superiors. Rather than drawing up battle plans, Wenck spends his days "like a visiting priest," checking in on the children and sick to make sure they have food and medicine.

Positioned west of Berlin, Wenck's Twelfth Army stood poised to fight. But the days passed, and the Russians encircled Berlin without any accompanying pincer movement by the Americans or British. So his Twelfth Army stands down. Unbeknownst to the men, their general is preparing to surrender to the Allies rather than let them fall into Russian hands.

True to form, Keitel shows up at Wenck's headquarters in his best uniform, complete with field marshal's baton.

"The battle for Berlin has begun," Keitel says somberly.

The field marshal then divulges a terrible secret: Wenck's army is Berlin's only hope. He orders the Twelfth to ignore any threat by the Americans and immediately turn in the opposite direction to save Berlin.

General Wenck has no time to plot. If he disobeys Keitel, he will be relieved of his command and most likely shot. Any hope of saving his men, who fondly call him Papi, will be lost. Yet if he follows the field marshal's order, his army will be destroyed by the Russians, and the refugees to whom he now devotes his days will be left to endure whatever horrors the Red Army wishes to impose.

There is no good outcome for Wenck. Yet Field Marshal Keitel demands an answer right now.

General Walther Wenck (right) was the youngest general in the German army. [Mary Evans Picture Library]

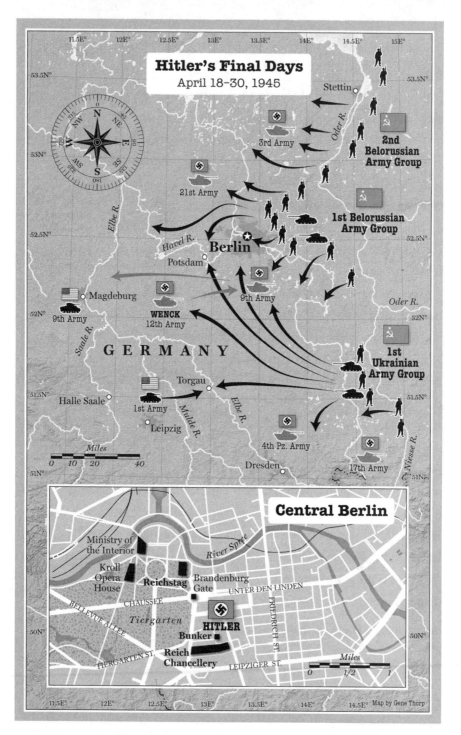

Hitler's Final Days
April 18–30, 1945

11.5E° 12E° 12.5E° 13E° 13.5E° 14E° 14.5E° 15E°

53.5N°

Stettin

3rd Army

2nd Belorussian Army Group

53N°

21st Army

1st Belorussian Army Group

52.5N°

Elbe R.

Havel R.

Berlin

Potsdam

Oder R.

52N°

Magdeburg

9th Army

WENCK 12th Army

9th Army

1st Ukrainian Army Group

GERMANY

Saale R.

Torgau

1st Army

Mulde R.

Elbe R.

51.5N°

Halle Saale

Leipzig

4th Pz. Army

Niesse R.

Miles

0 10 20 40

Dresden

17th Army

51N°

Central Berlin

Ministry of the Interior

Kroll Opera House

Reichstag

Brandenburg Gate

River Spree

UNTER DEN LINDEN

BELLEVUE ALLEE

CHAUSSEE

Tiergarten

HITLER Bunker

Reich Chancellery

FRIEDRICH ST.

TIERGARTEN ST.

LEIPZIGER ST.

Miles

0 1/2 1

50N°

11.5E° 12E° 12.5E° 13E° 13.5E° 14E° 14.5E°   Map by Gene Thorp

Map legend is on page x.

A member of the Hitler Youth learns to use a bazooka at a training camp in Germany. [Mary Evans Picture Library]

"Of course," Wenck tells him. "We will do as you order."

But General Walther Wenck is lying.

◆　◆　◆

Berlin is hopeless. Some 2.5 million Russians ring the city. They outnumber German soldiers three to one in men, tanks, aircraft,

[next pages] *Russian soldiers load Katyusha rocket launchers during the Russians' final advance into Berlin.* [Mary Evans Picture Library]

and artillery. The city's inner limits are defended by teenage Hitler Youth, the people's militia, and units of elderly Home Guardsmen. Few of them are battle-tested.

It will be a slaughter. Hordes of approaching Red Army soldiers, many of whom have marched a thousand miles to see their nation's flag raised over the capital of Germany, are eager to brutalize the German people.

Forty thousand Russian artillery guns hammer the city around the clock. Death screams down from all angles, filling the streets with rubble and setting homes ablaze. Berliners no longer pretend that life is normal. Thousands of refugees leave the city each day, hoping to find safety in the countryside. They walk, push their belongings in carts, and choke the roads in vehicles that are often abandoned for lack of gasoline. They sleep in churches, forests, abandoned railway cars, and any other space that keeps them relatively warm and dry. Everyone travels west. Only a fool would travel east, toward the lethal Russians.

For those who choose not to leave Berlin, the nightly ritual of sleeping in cellars and underground stations has become revolting. The smell of excrement and body odor makes these spaces appalling.

Aboveground, roving gangs of Nazi thugs and SS units travel from house to house, searching for deserters. The captured offenders are quickly hanged from light posts. Signs bearing the word TRAITOR are pinned to their chests, and their bodies are left to swing freely as a warning to others who might wish to quit the war prematurely.

At the notorious Lehrter Strasse prison, nothing stops the Nazi fanatics from finishing their dirty work. A special Gestapo contingent known as the *Sonderkommando* pretends that it is freeing political prisoners. As the men depart their cells, however, armed Gestapo agents fire bullets into the back of their necks.

There is no gas. There is no electricity. There is little food. German women kneel in the streets, butchering for meat workhorses that have been killed by Russian shelling. Other citizens seek food by trekking to the city's rail yards and breaking into freight trains, searching for canned goods and anything else that will fill their bellies.

Uniformed Hitler Youth members walk into grocery stores and demand food at gunpoint. "You are a godless youth, using American gangster methods," one woman screams at her nephew after she watches him terrorize a shopkeeper into giving him a hidden cache of food.

"Shut up," the Hitler Youth sneers. "It's now a matter of life and death."

No gun is needed to procure food in some parts of Berlin. Not wanting their supplies to fall into Russian hands, some shopkeepers give away everything on their shelves.

[next pages] *The injured and homeless line the streets of Russian-occupied Berlin.* [Mary Evans Picture Library]

A WEEK PASSES. THE BATTLE rages nonstop. Russian troops advance street by street, slowly taking control of the city. The young boys and old men enlisted as a last line of German defense now tear off their uniforms and armbands, frantically changing back into civilian clothing to avoid being murdered. Those who chose to stand and fight are now retreating into the heart of the city. An attempt to blow up vital bridges to stall the Russian advance ends in tragedy when an underground railway tunnel is mistakenly detonated. Inside are thousands of civilians and wounded soldiers trying to avoid the shelling aboveground. Rumors spread that hundreds drown as the four-mile-long tunnel floods with water.

Nazi leaflets litter the city, dropped from one of the few

Last-ditch efforts: Germans build tank defenses in Berlin. [Mary Evans Picture Library]

remaining Luftwaffe aircraft. "Persevere!" they read. "General Wenck and General Steiner are coming to the aid of Berlin."

Wenck has decided to try, although not how Nazi officials had hoped. He has turned Twelfth Army back toward Berlin—but keeps his positions on the Elbe—and surprises Russian forces near the suburb of Potsdam. But he is vastly outnumbered and can go no farther. Rather than fight onward, Wenck orders his troops to open a corridor from the city that will allow refugees and troops of the German Ninth Army to escape to the safety of the American lines. "It's not about Berlin anymore," he tells his soldiers as they turn their backs on the German capital. "It's not about the Reich anymore." In time, Wenck will push more than a hundred thousand German civilians and soldiers westward across the Elbe River, where he will surrender to American troops. The Russians chase the people in Wenck's long columns all the way to the American lines, attempting to kill them with artillery right up until the moment they cross the Elbe.

But even if General Wenck had succeeded in reaching central Berlin, there would be no stopping the Russians. Berlin is a city with 248 bridges, and only 120 have been destroyed as the Soviets penetrate closer and closer to the Führerbunker.

Russian troops cross pontoon bridges into Berlin, April 1945. [Mary Evans Picture Library]

CHAPTER 26

THE FÜHRERBUNKER

BERLIN, GERMANY ✠ APRIL 30, 1945 ✠ SHORTLY BEFORE 2 P.M.

THE FÜHRER IS SAYING FAREWELL. His personal staff lines up in the corridor outside his bedroom. Wearing a dark gray uniform jacket and creased black pants, Hitler shakes each hand and whispers a personal message to the two dozen secretaries, soldiers, and doctors who have tended to him during his three months in the bunker. They have all sworn an oath of loyalty to the Führer, but he releases them from that bond. He gives them permission to leave the bunker immediately and flee to the American lines, should they choose.

Throughout it all, Eva Braun stands at the Führer's side, wearing a black dress with pink roses framing the square neckline. She has chosen this dress because it is Hitler's favorite. Her blond hair is washed and perfectly styled, as befitting her new position of Nazi Germany's first lady.

Almost exactly three years earlier, Hitler celebrates his birthday with Eva Braun and guests. [Mary Evans Picture Library]

After the Führer speaks with secretary Traudl Junge, Eva pulls her close and whispers in her ear: "Please do try to get out. You may yet make it through."

Eva Braun, of course, is not leaving. She has just sworn the ultimate loyalty oath to the Führer—yesterday they were married. These same staff members had gathered to celebrate the wedding of Adolf Hitler and Eva Braun. Glasses of champagne were filled. Only the Führer did not partake. The mood was outwardly joyous, but there was a somber tone to the proceedings. Marriage is normally a time of hope for the future. But one and all know that Adolf Hitler and Eva Braun will soon kill themselves.

General Walther Wenck and his Twelfth Army will never save Berlin. The Soviet army is close by. Its advance units are just five hundred yards away from the Führerbunker, and they now shell the compound from their positions in the Tiergarten, the sprawling park in the heart of the city, where Eva Braun once delighted in afternoons of target practice with her pistol. Many of the trees there are now mere splinters. Yet those still standing bear the first blooms of spring—signs of life that contrast sharply with the nearby Reichstag building and Kroll Opera House, both battered and pocked by artillery, a reminder that the once proud city of Berlin is soon to die.

Adolf Hitler has filled the bunker's corridors with talk of suicide for the last ten days, pragmatically stating that the only other option is to become a Russian prisoner—and for the Führer, that fate is no option at all. Eva Braun, of course, would be a similar trophy if the Russians took her alive, so she, too, must die by her own hand. Earlier today she chose not to have a dentist examine a sore tooth, laughing that it soon wouldn't matter anyway. And she surprised Traudl Junge just a few hours ago by giving her a fur coat made of silver fox. Eva's initials were sewn onto the lining inside the well-known symbol of good luck: a four-leaf clover.

Hitler plans to kill himself with a cyanide pill. Until recently he was frightened that it would not work. So he ordered that a similar pill be tested on his beloved dog, Blondi, the German shepherd who has been by his side for much of the war. Her jaws were pried open by Sergeant Fritz Tornow, the Führer's dog handler. A pair of pliers containing a capsule of hydrogen cyanide, the liquid form of cyanide, was placed in her mouth by Dr. Werner Haase, the professor who devised Hitler's own unique suicide technique.

Blondi is a large dog, seen by the Führer as a symbol of German pride because she resembles a wolf. But she trusts her master and allows Haase to press the pliers together, breaking the capsule and spilling the acid onto her tongue.

Blondi dies instantly.

Dr. Haase immediately calls for Hitler so that he might see for himself the pill's effectiveness. The Führer is speechless at the sight of Blondi lying motionless on the floor. He takes one look and leaves, going directly to his bedroom.

Now it's his turn.

After dismissing the staff, Hitler and Eva retire to his sitting room and close the door. Eva Braun sits down on the end of the couch, resting her head on the arm as if she is lying down to take a nap.

Hitler has been carrying his Walther 7.65mm pistol for the past few weeks, and now he chambers a round. History does not record the final words between Adolf Hitler and Eva Braun. They have known each other for sixteen years. She has seen him rise to power, just as she now sees his physical decline and the end of his dreams of power.

Eva is curled up like a cat on the right side of the sofa. Adolf Hitler takes a seat on the other end, pistol in hand. Eva's own revolver rests on a nearby table, next to a vase of flowers.

She goes first, sliding the cyanide pill out of the small brass lipstick-size vial and placing it between her teeth. She rests her head on the armrest again and bites down on the capsule.

To prevent the possibility of failure, Eva is now meant to place her small handgun to her temple and finish the job. But Eva has already made it clear she will not shoot herself. "I want to be a beautiful corpse," she insisted to Hitler.

The bunker sitting room immediately smells of bitter almond, a scent commonly associated with cyanide. Eva Braun's body loses the ability to absorb oxygen. Her heart and brain, the two organs that need air the most, shut down in an instant. It is a death not unlike that suffered by the millions of Jews her new husband sent to the gas chambers. The Zyklon B gas that was used in the death camps is also a form of cyanide.

Seconds later, still curled up in the fetal position, Eva Braun is dead.

The Führer then places his capsule between his teeth. At the same time, he points the gun at his right temple. He bites down and pulls the trigger a split second later.

His body sags to the side, until his torso hangs limp against Eva Braun's. The Führer's pistol drops to the floor next to his foot. Blood pours from his shattered skull, dripping off the couch, forming a great crimson puddle on the floor.

Adolf Hitler, the man who murdered millions, has claimed his last victim.

Russian artillery battle their way into Berlin.
[Mary Evans Picture Library]

THE BATTLE OF BERLIN

I T WAS 12:45 ON THE morning of April 23, 1945, when German Field Marshal Wilhelm Keitel announced to General Walther Wenck that "the battle for Berlin has begun." The city is now encircled by Soviet troops. Within the city, General Helmuth Weidling has about forty-five thousand men, boys, and veterans left. The days pass, and the Russians continue to strangle Berlin. There is no accompanying pincer movement by the Americans or British. It appears that the Soviets have the city to themselves. In fact, the western Allied armies have made an agreement that they will stay back from Berlin, although they are only sixty miles away, and let the Soviets take the city.

One thousand miles east, in Moscow, Joseph Stalin has foreseen the fall of Berlin. He signs a directive known as Stavka 11074, dictating that the First Belorussian and First Ukrainian armies will divide the city between them. Of his top generals, it will be

Marshal Georgy K. Zhukov, the hero of Stalingrad and the Battle of Moscow, who will get the honor of hoisting the Soviet flag atop the German Reichstag, the German parliament building.

Stalin's power is at its pinnacle. He has sent twenty armies, 6,300 tanks, and 7,500 aircraft to subdue Berlin. He has ordered that no brutality be spared the Germans. He wants maximum suffering inflicted.

There is no normal life in Berlin now. Food is short; homes are reduced to rubble; streets are filthy. People crouch in tunnels and churches to avoid bombings. The worst, however, is on the way. And as bad as the people of Berlin believe it will be, the truth will be far worse. The stories of the Russian soldiers' brutality will become legendary.

On April 30, the day that Adolf Hitler and Eva Braun committed suicide, the mortar and shell assaults intensified on

A Russian soldier poses with the Soviet flag on top of the Reichstag.
[Mary Evans Picture Library]

the Reichstag. At 10:50 that night a huge Soviet flag, depicting the hammer and sickle, was placed on the rooftop. (The next day the placement was reenacted for photographers.)

At 6 A.M. on Wednesday, May 2, General Helmuth Weidling, the commander of the Berlin defense, walks across the front lines and surrenders to the Soviets. A German eyewitness recalls that "vans with loudspeakers drove through the streets ordering us to cease all resistance. Suddenly shooting and bombing stopped and the unreal silence meant one ordeal was over for us and another was about to begin."

An estimated 80,000 Russians died or were missing after the Battle of Berlin. Civilian casualties are difficult to place, but it is estimated that 80,000 to 125,000 citizens of Berlin were killed. The number of German military casualties is a matter of debate. Early Soviet estimates were 460,000 killed and 480,000 captured, but later German estimates say 92,000 to 100,000 died.

On May 2, 1945, General Helmuth Weidling, commander of the Berlin defense effort, emerges from a bunker to formally surrender. [Mary Evans Picture Library]

AFTERWORD

THE BODIES OF GERMAN FÜHRER **Adolf Hitler** and his wife, **Eva Braun**, were immediately wrapped in blankets and taken aboveground to be burned. Hitler was afraid that his corpse might otherwise become an exhibit in a Russian museum. Forty gallons of gasoline were used for the incineration. The Soviets confirmed the identity of the bodies within two weeks, but for years pretended to know nothing about Hitler's fate.

U.S. General George Patton, commander of the Third Army, died on December 21, 1945, as the result of a car accident earlier in the month in Mannheim, Germany. He had been serving as commander of the Fifteenth Army in American-occupied Germany. He is buried at the American Cemetery just outside Luxembourg City with thousands of Third Army soldiers who fell during the Battle of the Bulge and in the advance to the Rhine. Patton's

An American soldier examines gasoline canisters that litter the ground above the bunker where Hitler and Eva Braun lived. [Mary Evans Picture Library]

burial site became such a popular postwar attraction that the horde of visitors trampled the nearby graves. So on March 19, 1947, his body was exhumed and moved to the location where it now rests, in a solitary spot apart from the long rows of white crosses, at the very front of the cemetery. The location suggests that Patton is still leading his men.

The casket containing the body of General Patton is carried by an army half-track to a U.S. military cemetery in Hamm, Germany. [Associated Press]

U.S. General Dwight Eisenhower, supreme commander of the Allied forces in Europe, returned home a hero. He did not believe that a military officer should interest himself in politics, so despite widespread popular support for an Eisenhower presidential candidacy in 1948, he accepted a position as head of Columbia University in New York City rather than run for office. However, he soon changed his mind. He was elected president of the United States in 1952 and served two terms. When doctors told him that his chain smoking was a hazard to his health, Eisenhower quit his four-packs-a-day habit cold turkey. He died of heart failure on March 28, 1969, at seventy-eight years of age.

Thirty-fourth president of the United States Dwight D. Eisenhower arrives for a meeting in London, 1959.
[Mary Evans Picture Library]

A formal portrait of General Omar Bradley.
[Mary Evans Picture Library]

U.S. General Omar Bradley, commander of the Twelfth Army Group, continued to serve until August 1953, first as army chief of staff and eventually rising to the rank of five-star general. As the first chairman of the Joint Chiefs of Staff, Bradley provided military advice in the Korean War. In civilian life, he consulted with President Lyndon Johnson during the Vietnam War. Bradley died in 1981 at age eighty-eight.

British Prime Minister Winston Churchill enjoyed a long life. Though he was overweight, a heavy drinker, and rarely seen without a cigar, Britain's wartime prime minister lived to be ninety. He died on January 24, 1965. Churchill's funeral was the largest state ceremony in world history at that time, with delegates from 112 nations attending to pay their respects. As a wooden boat carried his casket down the Thames River, the dock cranes lining the waterway lowered their jibs in salute.

Prime Minister Winston Churchill gives his customary "V for Victory" sign.
[Mary Evans Picture Library]

Russian leader and military commander Joseph Stalin. [Mary Evans Picture Library]

Russian dictator Joseph Stalin ruled the Soviet Union for nearly thirty years, dying in 1953 at the age of seventy-three from a brain hemorrhage. His body was embalmed and placed in a mausoleum next to that of Vladimir Lenin, founder of the Soviet Union. It was on public display for eight years in Moscow's Red Square until October 31, 1961, when Stalin's remains were moved to the Kremlin Wall necropolis.

German General Walther Wenck, commander of the Twelfth Army, was arrested and held as a prisoner of war by the Americans until 1947. He died in 1982 following an automobile crash. He was eighty-one years old.

German Field Marshal Wilhelm Keitel, Hitler's commander of the armed forces, was tried at the Nuremberg war crime trials, found guilty, and hanged on October 16, 1946.

The day after Adolf Hitler and Eva Braun died, **Reich Minister of Propaganda Joseph Goebbels** and his wife, Magda, poisoned their six children and then committed suicide.

General Wilhelm Keitel in his prison cell at the International Military Tribunal in Nuremberg, Germany. [National Archives and Records Administration, College Park]

Heinrich Himmler, head of the SS, betrayed Hitler in the last days of the war by sending a message to Eisenhower suggesting negotiations for surrender. One of the last things Hitler did before he committed suicide was to strip Himmler of his rank. Himmler disguised himself and acquired papers in another name. After he was arrested by the Russians and turned over to the British, he confessed his identity. He committed suicide on May 23, 1945, by biting a cyanide pill he had hidden on his person.

Reichsführer of the SS Heinrich Himmler. [United States Holocaust Memorial Museum, courtesy of James Blevins]

Martin Bormann, head of the Nazi Party chancellery, died while fleeing Berlin. His remains were not positively identified until 1973, so many people thought he had escaped. Bormann was tried in absentia at Nuremberg and sentenced to death.

Martin Bormann, head of the Nazi Party Chancellery. [National Archives and Records Administration, College Park]

At his trial in Nuremberg, **German Minister of Armaments Albert Speer** admitted to using slave labor at the munitions factories he controlled. Speer was sentenced to twenty years in prison. When he got out, he wrote a bestselling book, *Inside the Third Reich.* He died in London on September 1, 1981.

Albert Speer on trial at Nuremberg. [Harry S. Truman Library, United States Holocaust Memorial Museum, courtesy of Robert Jackson and Robert Kempner]

U.S. General George Marshall, the man who served as army chief of staff and general of the army during the war, died in Washington, D.C., in 1959 at the age of seventy-eight. In his lifetime, he served as secretary of state and secretary of defense. He was *Time* magazine's Man of the Year twice and won the 1953 Nobel Peace Prize. His most enduring legacy was the Marshall Plan, which allowed Europe to rebuild after the war with financial assistance from the United States. President Harry Truman once said that Marshall was the greatest man of World War II.

General George Marshall in 1947. [Mary Evans Picture Library]

British Field Marshal Bernard Law Montgomery was named First Viscount Montgomery of Alamein after the war, a title referring to his epic defeat of Field Marshal Erwin Rommel in the Egyptian desert. Montgomery served as Britain's chief of the Imperial General Staff from 1946 to 1948 and deputy commander of the North Atlantic Treaty Organization from 1951 to 1958, when he retired at the age of seventy-one. He died in 1976 at age eighty-eight.

Field Marshal Bernard Law Montgomery. [Mary Evans Picture Library]

U.S. Lieutenant Colonel Creighton "Abe" Abrams had a long and successful military career. He went on to become a four-star general and chief of staff of the army during the Vietnam War. Abrams's lifelong fondness for cigars caught up with him, and he died of complications from lung cancer surgery in 1974, just shy of his sixtieth birthday.

U.S. Brigadier General Anthony McAuliffe, the hero of Bastogne, would never shake his connection with the "Nuts" response, which has gone down in history as one of wartime's great quotations. His military career continued until 1956, when he retired and went into industry. He recounted his weariness about his claim to fame: "One evening a dear old Southern lady invited me to dinner. I had a delightful time talking to her and her charming guests. I was pleased because no mention was made the entire evening of the 'nuts' incident. As I prepared to depart and thanked my hostess for an enjoyable evening, she replied, 'Thank you and good night, General McNut.'" He died in 1975 at the age of seventy-seven.

General Anthony McAuliffe in Bastogne, Belgium. [Alamy]

THE RISE OF HITLER
AND THE NAZI PARTY

ADOLF HITLER (1889–1945) WAS BORN IN Austria. An indifferent student, Hitler was allowed to leave school and pursue studies in the arts; he dreamed of becoming an architect. When World War I began, Hitler applied to join the German army and was accepted. He spent the war years behind the front lines, carrying messages for powerful commanders.

Perhaps the seeds for his anti-Semitism and intolerance can be found in this letter he wrote during the war: "Those of us who are lucky enough to see our homeland again will find it purer and cleansed of affections for foreigners."

After the war, Hitler worked as an intelligence officer, reporting on the activities of Germany's many small political parties. The party he felt most akin to was the German Workers' Party, founded

Young Nazi supporters stand next to a sign that reads, "Adolf Hitler will provide work and bread!" Behind them are posters urging women and workers to vote for the Nazi Party. [Stadtarchiv Rosenheim]

in 1919 with a platform of nationalism and anti-Semitism. Hitler began to speak in cafés and taverns about his extreme nationalistic views. He was a very good speaker, the kind of person whom people found mesmerizing. Within six months, Hitler convinced leaders to add "National Socialist" to the party name, and two years later, he was the leader of the Nazi Party.

Hitler decided that the party needed a new flag, something striking that would look good both large on a poster and small on a uniform patch. In his autobiography, *Mein Kampf*, Hitler describes the Nazis' new flag: "In red we see the social idea of the movement, in white the nationalistic idea, in the swastika the mission of the struggle for the victory of the Aryan man, and, by the same token, the victory of the idea of creative work, which as such always has been and always will be anti-Semitic." The swastika is a centuries-old symbol that, before its use by the Nazis, meant life and good luck.

As a result of the Versailles Treaty that ended

A balcony hung with Nazi flags and the flag of Imperial Germany, 1933. [Mary Evans Picture Library]

World War I, Germany was required to pay more money that it had in reparations, and its citizens suffered wide-scale unemployment. As people worried about their livelihoods, many became attracted to politicians who had radical, forceful views and spoke with conviction about how their plans would solve the problems of the citizens. Hitler, representing the Nazi Party, had such conviction. He ran for president of Germany in 1932 and came in second. The winner, Paul von Hindenburg, named Adolf Hitler as head of a coalition government in 1933, a position called chancellor.

Using the power of the chancellor, Hitler pressured the parliament to pass the Enabling Act, which allowed him to ignore the constitution and gave his decrees the power of law. He forced the other political parties to disband. After von Hindenburg's death in 1934, Hitler appointed himself president and chancellor.

Beginning on April 7, 1933, German law required that obtaining a certificate of racial purity was mandatory for any individual wishing to hold public office in Germany or to gain membership in the Nazi Party. The Nazis prized people who were Aryan, thought to be of Nordic and Germanic ethnicity. The defining characteristics of Aryans were blue eyes, blond hair, a tall, strong physique, and Caucasian skin pigment. The Aryan bloodline was thought to be purer because it had not mingled with that of other ethnicities. Even top-level military officers had to prove their racial purity by providing

Hitler would take over the German government from
Paul von Hindenburg (left), 1933. [Mary Evans Picture Library]

*A Jewish family, wearing the required Star of David badges,
is deported from a ghetto in 1939.* [Mary Evans Picture Library]

records of their family lineage dating back to 1750. This practice of achieving racial superiority was based on "scientific racism," which suggested that some races were more advanced than others. Further laws allowed for the sterilization of people deemed unworthy of propagating the German race and banned marriage between Jews and Germans.

Hitler's anti-Semitic policies led hundreds of thousands of Jewish citizens to emigrate from Germany, a number that included 83 percent of all German Jews under the age of twenty-one. But no more were allowed to leave once war was declared.

Germany invaded Poland on September 1, 1939. England and France promptly declared war on Germany. World War II had begun. On January 30, 1942, Hitler told the German people, "This war can end two ways. Either the extermination of the Aryan peoples or the disappearance of Jewry from Europe."

Now trapped in Germany and the countries the Nazis occupied, the remaining Europeans of Jewish ancestry were being systematically rounded up and murdered. Dachau—the first concentration camp, opened in 1933 to house political prisoners—soon evolved into a death camp.

The Nazi Party was outlawed at the end of World War II. Many of its most powerful members were brought to trial and sentenced for the deaths of an estimated six million Jews and four to six million other enemies of the state, such as Roma (gypsies), homosexuals, and disabled people.

THE SYMBOL OF THE SWASTIKA

FOR THOUSANDS OF YEARS BEFORE the rise of the Nazi Party, the swastika was a symbol of good and of the sun. It comes from a Sanskrit word, *svastika*, which means "to be well." Found in ancient cultures all over the world—including ancient Troy of 1000 B.C., Tibet, Greece, Africa, India, China, and Native American faiths—its meaning has largely been changed by its association with Hitler and the Nazi Party.

Some nineteenth-century Germans believed that the swastika represented pure Aryan identity. They began to use it on magazines and posters as a secret symbol of nationalistic theories. Hitler thought the symbol would look dramatic on the flag of the Nazi Party. On August 7, 1920, it was adopted by a Nazi Party conference.

Buddhists and Hindus continue to use the shape of the swastika in their art and building decoration to mean infinity and life.

HITLER'S STATURE, HEALTH, AND DIET

ADOLF HITLER STOOD FIVE FEET eight inches high and weighed approximately 160 to 165 pounds.

Although it is impossible to know for certain, it seems that Adolf Hitler suffered illnesses from his youth. He is known to have complained of stomach cramps and had a lung infection that kept him out of high school for a time.

It seems clear to many researchers that Hitler suffered from idiopathic Parkinson's disease. *Idiopathic* simply means that the cause of the disease is unknown. People with Parkinson's disease experience tremors, rigidity, and slowness of movement. Eyewitnesses describe Hitler as shaking so much he couldn't hold a fork, having to move his right arm with his left to position it, and walking hunched over. For many people, Parkinson's eventually leads to memory loss. By late September 1944, Hitler's memory had begun to deteriorate; he could not remember some people's names.

Hitler also suffered from insomnia; eye problems that made him sensitive to bright light; severe, chronic stomach cramps; and eczema, an itchy, scaly skin condition.

As a result of the assassination attempt on July 20, 1944, when a bomb exploded near his desk, Hitler's right eardrum was ruptured and his right arm was temporarily paralyzed. Some medical historians believe that Dr. Theo Morrell, whom Hitler began to see in 1937 and later said he could not live without, injected Hitler with methamphetamines and other drugs with a frequency that gradually made him an addict. We shall never know.

During his years as Führer, several women were forced to work as food tasters for Hitler. In 2013, one woman, then ninety-five years old, told a British newspaper: "It was all vegetarian, the most delicious fresh things, from asparagus to peppers and peas, served with rice and salads. It was all arranged on one plate, just as it was served to him. There was no meat, and I do not remember any fish."

It is possible that, as Hitler aged, he adopted a vegetarian diet, perhaps because he felt it increased a body's purity.

THE TOOTHBRUSH MUSTACHE

HITLER'S TINY MUSTACHE HAS BECOME a symbol of evil. But this was not Hitler's first mustache style. Early photographs show him to be clean shaven, then later with a bushy mustache that turned up at the ends, and finally with the postage-size mustache under his nose.

Some fashion historians say that Americans brought the style to Europe. Certainly Charlie Chaplin wore one as early as 1915, and he was by then a very famous actor. In Europe, several famous sports figures wore small mustaches, as did upper-class men in Berlin and Vienna.

No one knows why Hitler adopted the style. Some say he was told to shave his bushy mustache during World War I because it impeded the seal of his regulation gas mask. Others assume he looked at rich, powerful men and wanted to emulate them.

GERMAN SOLDIERS AND POLICE: THE WEHRMACHT, SS, AND GESTAPO

THE DIFFERENCES BETWEEN THE WEHRMACHT and the SS can be summed up in the translations of their names. Wehrmacht means "defense force" in German, while the SS, or *Schutzstaffel*, roughly translates to "protection squadron"—as in, the protection of Adolf Hitler and the Nazi Party ideology.

The Wehrmacht comprised all of the German armed forces— the *Heer* (army), *Kriegsmarine* (navy), and *Luftwaffe* (air force)—as well as the SS. Each wore different uniforms, the SS often with *SS* on the collar or in camouflage. Though a branch of the military, SS troopers swore to be loyal to Adolf Hitler unto death; they could be ordered to do literally anything in the name of the Führer. This led SS troopers to commit scores of unconscionable acts of terror and brutality—acts that included murdering prisoners of war, Jews, and other innocent civilians. The *Totenkopf* (skull and crossbones) worn on SS headgear signified that "you shall always be

A ceremonial march of SS soldiers precedes a meeting where Hitler will give a speech. [Mary Evans Picture Library]

willing to put yourself at stake for the life of the whole community," in the words of SS leader Heinrich Himmler.

The barbaric behavior of the SS at the concentration camps stands in sharp contrast to the behavior of Wehrmacht soldiers such as Field Marshal Erwin Rommel, whose troops were forbidden from ill treatment of civilians. Rommel and other German commanders ignored SS admonitions to murder Jews and enemy prisoners. That said, many German fighting men participated in civilian atrocities, especially against the peoples of Poland, France, and the Soviet Union. "I have come to know there is a real difference between the regular German soldier and officer, and Hitler and his criminal group," Dwight Eisenhower later said. "The German soldier as such has not lost his honor. The fact that certain individuals committed in war dishonorable and despicable acts reflects on the individuals concerned, and not on the great majority of German soldiers and officers."

The Gestapo was a branch of the SS also under the supervision of Heinrich Himmler. As Germany's official secret police (and often clad in civilian clothing), Gestapo agents terrorized and murdered anyone who might represent a threat to the Nazi Party. Even law-abiding Germans lived in fear of a visit from the Gestapo because its officers operated outside the normal laws of state. The Gestapo headquarters featured underground cells where prisoners were held before being tortured. Today the remains of those cells lie beneath the Topography of Terror historic site in Berlin, which is built on the large city block that was once home to the Gestapo. The buildings comprising Himmler's headquarters have been demolished. All traces of that awful legacy have been replaced by a stark landscape of gray stones. Except for the documentation center and the legacy of murder represented by the excavated cellar rooms of the SS headquarters, the entire city block will never again be developed.

The ruins of the Gestapo headquarters in Berlin, photographed in 1948.
[Mary Evans Picture Library]

JOSEPH STALIN
AND THE RUSSIAN ARMY

THE RUSSIANS WERE UNEASY PARTNERS with the United States and western European countries. Joseph Stalin, premier of the Soviet Union, was both a dictator and a communist. He had initially signed a nonagression pact with Germany, and Russia had been supplying Germany with much-needed oil and wheat. All that stopped when Germany invaded Russia.

On June 22, 1941, using more than three million troops, nineteen panzer divisions, three thousand tanks, twenty-five hundred aircraft, and seven thousand artillery pieces, Hitler attacked the country he had asked to join the Axis powers just one month before. In his quest for world domination, Hitler saw that besides the United States, which was neutral at the time, and England, which was winning the air war with Germany, his biggest threat was Russia in the east. To fight the largest army in the world, Germany would have to rely on its skill at the blitzkrieg—quickly destroying enemy air power early in the invasion, disabling communications systems, and infiltrating behind enemy lines to surround them. And the Germans accomplished many of these goals. In the first day, the Germans destroyed or disabled a thousand Russian aircraft. In only a few days, they had advanced three hundred miles into Russia and were heading for Moscow.

Then Hitler changed his strategy. He decided to concentrate his invasion forces on southern Russia and Ukraine to gain access to their economic resources. Only after Ukraine was secure did he allow his troops to march on Moscow that fall. By December 1941 the Germans were twenty miles from the Kremlin, but the onset

A German panzer unit advances into Russia, July 1941.
[Mary Evans Picture Library]

of winter and fresh Russian troops from Siberia stalled their advance.

In 1942, Hitler launched a two-pronged attack, sending one set of troops to Baku, a region rich in oil, and another toward Stalingrad. In Stalingrad, the German soldiers discovered brutal, ferocious opponents who fought to kill, often at close range. The Red Army, as the Russians were called, had recovered from its initial losses and disorganization and soundly defeated the Germans in a battle that lasted from July 1942 to February 1943.

After the Battle of Stalingrad, the German forces retreated. The Russians had earned their reputation for violence and abuse, but so did the Germans. During the time they occupied Russian villages, there were tales of brutal oppression, starvation, and violence. As the Russians chased the

Soldiers fight house-to-house during the Battle of Stalingrad, Russia, 1942–1943.
[Mary Evans Picture Library]

Germans to their border, Hitler issued an order for German citizens to destroy anything the Russians might use.

By 1943, the Russians had been fighting the Nazis on Soviet soil for two years. Stalin needed his Allies to take some pressure off his army by drawing German efforts elsewhere. Though England and the United States agreed to attack Sicily and open a front in Europe, Stalin continued to push for a larger invasion in the north.

With the German army's assets further divided after D-day in June 1944, Russia succeeded in entering Eastern Europe, taking parts of Bulgaria, Romania, Poland, Lithuania, Latvia, and Estonia. By April 1945, the Red Army accomplished the siege of Berlin, effectively ending the war in Europe.

It is estimated that, out of a population of 168 million Soviets, twenty million soldiers and civilians died between June 22, 1941, and May 2, 1945.

The uneasy relationship between Russia and the western Allies became increasingly strained over disagreements about the governance of postwar Europe. The growing mistrust between the United States and the Soviet Union ultimately resulted in the Cold War.

THE RED BALL EXPRESS

LARGE ARMIES ON THE MOVE need constant sources of supplies: food, fuel, ammunition, replacement clothing, and medicine. As General Patton planned his march through France and then on to Germany, an essential element was the establishment of a trucking operation. On August 21, 1944, the Red Ball Express was founded. A code name given by the Army Transportation Corps, "red ball" referred to the railroad symbol for express freight.

The supply routes were expected to be clear of civilian traffic, but trucks could not zip along at high speeds. The roads were poor and narrow. Drivers hoped to maintain a speed of twenty-five miles per hour and were instructed to keep sixty yards between trucks. (At that distance, if a bomb fell, perhaps only one or two trucks would be lost.) At night, a blackout was enforced. Trucks could only use "cat eyes," headlight covers that allowed just a slit of light to shine through.

As many as nine hundred trucks were on the road at the same time, making round trips of fifty-four hours. It was 350 miles to Patton's Third Army from Saint-Lô in Normandy. "When General Patton said for you to be there, you were there if you had to drive all day and all night. If those trucks broke down, we'd fix them and they'd run again," said James D. Rookard, a driver with the Red Ball Express.

Nearly 75 percent of the drivers were African American. Even though most black soldiers were relegated to behind-the-scenes jobs at that time, this unique group was essential to the front lines.

During an eighty-two-day mission, the Red Ball drivers delivered 412,193 tons of supplies.

With the reconstruction of French railway lines, the need for the Red Ball Express diminished, and it was disbanded November 16, 1944. However, many of its drivers went on to help Patton turn his Third Army toward Bastogne and the Battle of the Bulge.

Members of the Red Ball Express repair a truck while a crewman keeps watch.
[Army Transportation Museum]

THE EAGLE'S NEST

FOR THE FÜHRER'S FIFTIETH BIRTHDAY, the Nazi government hired four thousand workers to build a mountaintop château. This lavish building, meant for diplomatic receptions as well as Hitler's private enjoyment, rises atop a mountain in the Bavarian Alps. The nearest village, Berchtesgaden, is where Hitler wrote the second volume of his autobiography, *Mein Kampf*, or "My Struggle." Several of his closest advisers also had homes in the area.

Visitors approached the Eagle's Nest by way of a twisting road passing through five tunnels cut out of the mountain. From the parking area, a tunnel into the rock face led to an elevator that took them up the final four hundred feet. There they might be shown to a dining room that could seat thirty people, eat with silverware engraved with Hitler's initials, and admire a fireplace covered in red marble that had been presented to the Führer by his ally Benito Mussolini of Italy. The most frequent visitor to the house was not

Hitler but his mistress, Eva Braun. The Führer had an aversion to heights and regularly expressed concerns over the elevator's safety.

American and French soldiers visit the ruins of the Eagle's Nest on May 4, 1945. [Mary Evans Picture Library]

As the war came to a close, and millions of American and British troops were in Germany, the Eagle's Nest became a popular tourist attraction. As many as three thousand visited each weekday—and three times that many on weekends. Soldiers looted anything they could find to save as souvenirs.

INSIDE HITLER'S BUNKER

AMERICAN BOMBERS SWEPT OVER BERLIN on February 3, 1945, in one of hundreds of raids that would level the city. The target this day was the inner city, where government offices and ministries were located. The Reich Chancellery, Hitler's official office and apartment, was in the bombers sights. The damage that day, including the destruction from fire bombs that hit Hitler's apartment, was extensive. But Hitler and his staff had already moved to the bunker below the grounds.

The bunker was originally an air-raid shelter. It had evolved into a two-level warren of conference rooms, bedrooms, a kitchen and dining room, an infirmary, and offices. In one corner of the bunker, rising above the ground level, was an observation tower. Above the bunker, in the park that surrounded the chancellery, antitank guns and mortars kept guard. Between February and April, Hitler would occasionally step out of the bunker to walk Blondi in the park.

The bunker was a bleak place to live and work. The walls were gray concrete; there was very little decoration anywhere except in the anteroom to Hitler's apartment; and the artificial light made everyone look pale and unhealthy. A diesel generator between the floors supplied light, fresh air, water pumps, and heat.

For two and a half months, Hitler's closest advisers lived here, too. Hitler met with his staff in his conference room for hours every day, plotting a potential victory for the Third Reich.

The first level, or Vorbunker, held offices for mapmakers, radio operators, secretaries, as well as bedrooms, an infirmary, and a kitchen and dining room. Down a spiral staircase were Hitler's private quarters and a conference room.

A third area of the complex housed the garage bunker and rooms for drivers.

NAZI CASH, ART,
AND STOLEN POSSESSIONS

AFTER CROSSING THE RHINE RIVER in March 1945, Allied soldiers spanned across Germany, fighting their way toward Berlin. They checked every hay barn, small country lane, abandoned house, church, cave, and underground mine for German snipers. They fought to capture each town as they advanced. It was slow, often frightening work that occupied millions of soldiers as the war drew to a close. They also interviewed citizens and workers about the areas they traveled through.

At Merkers, Germany, a town two hundred miles southwest of Berlin, civilians told U.S. soldiers that they had heard about great quantities of gold stored in the salt mine there. This information traveled up the chain of command. The first examination of the mine showed a thick brick wall with a heavy vault door. Permission was given to blast the door open.

Inside was an almost unimaginable scene: rows and rows of gold bars packaged together, bags of currency from many

European countries. A partial inventory showed that there were 8,198 bars of gold bullion; fifty-five boxes of crated gold bullion; hundreds of bags of gold items; more than 1,300 bags of gold Reichsmarks, British gold pounds, and French gold francs; 711 bags of American twenty-dollar gold pieces; and hundreds of bags of foreign paper currency.

The gold had been delivered to the mine for safekeeping once the Allies started carrying out constant bombing sorties, almost leveling the German central bank, the Reichsbank in Berlin. The Germans needed the money to pay soldiers, buy supplies for the vast army, and keep the country's economy stable. Included in the stash were gold and currency looted from banks in Europe during the Nazi drive west.

As the mine and its tunnels were further explored, soldiers discovered bags of personal property taken from victims in the death camps as well as valuable artwork from German museums. It was eventually determined that one-fourth of the holdings of fourteen museums was at the Merkers mine.

General Eisenhower visited the mine on April 12, 1945, with Generals Bradley and Patton. With them

U.S. soldiers examine Édouard Manet's painting "In the Conservatory" on April 25, 1945. It rests on wheeled carts that moved salt out of the mine when it was in operation. [National Archives]

were photographers from the Signal Corps and news reporters to document the discovery. Eisenhower decided to move the treasure out of the mine and further to the rear to protect it, to develop a thorough inventory, and to free up the soldiers who were guarding the mine to return to active fighting on the front. Eleven thousand containers traveled by truck to Frankfurt, with constant protection from aircraft.

Treasure was discovered in other caves and mines in the region—in Siegen, Ransbach, and Bernterode. In an old salt mine in Altaussee, Austria, Hitler had stashed artwork stolen from museums, churches, and private homes in his drive across Europe. He had grand plans to build a museum in Linz, Austria, where he had lived as a child, to showcase the art and to stand as a monument to his reign. That stash and its discovery and rescue are explored in the books *The Rape of Europa* by Lynn H. Nicholas and *The Monuments Men* by Robert M. Edsel, and in the subsequent documentary and feature films with the same names. Each tells the story of members of the Monuments, Fine Arts, and Archives Section of the Allied army, whose job it was to save as much plundered art as possible and to prevent, if possible, the bombing of historic sites.

After the war, some of the monies stolen from European banks were returned to them. It took until 1998 for the commission set up after the war to complete the dispersal of the gold. At the end, there was about sixty million dollars left. The countries that had claims to the money agreed to give it to the Nazi Persecutee Relief Fund, which provides aid to people who were victims of the Nazis.

A U.S. soldier inspects art and other loot stored in a church in Ellingen, Germany, on April 24, 1945. [National Archives]

CONCENTRATION CAMPS:
AUSCHWITZ-BIRKENAU

THE NAZIS BUILT TWENTY THOUSAND camps beginning in 1933. Some were labor camps, where prisoners were held as slaves and forced to work in factory jobs, producing goods for the war effort. Others were POW (prisoner-of-war) camps for captured soldiers. And some were built with the express purpose of exterminating people.

While the term "concentration camp" is widely used to describe the many places where the Nazis tortured and killed their enemies, real and imagined, six facilities—Chelmno, Belzec, Sobibor, Treblinka, Majdanek, and Auschwitz-Birkenau—also carried the term "extermination camp" because most prisoners were murdered immediately upon arrival. Auschwitz-Birkenau served the dual purpose of forced labor and extermination.

There were five crematoriums at Auschwitz. Each had a room for gassing victims and ovens for burning the bodies. When the number of bodies became too much for the ovens to handle, the

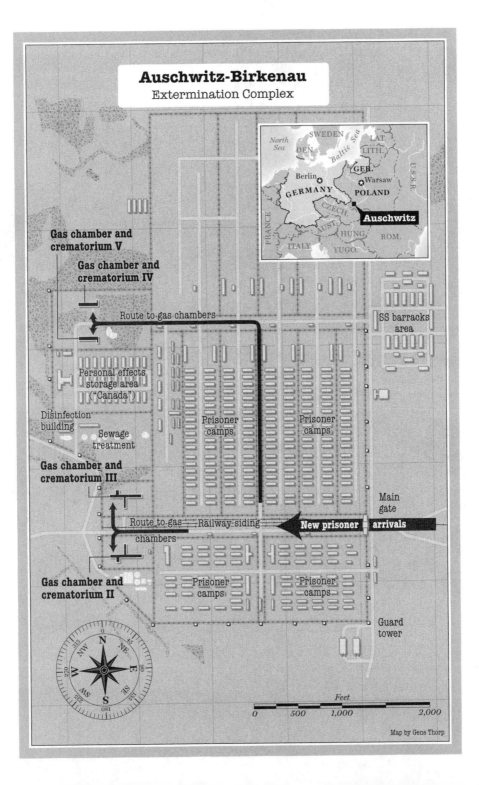

Auschwitz-Birkenau
Extermination Complex

Gas chamber and crematorium V

Gas chamber and crematorium IV

Route to gas chambers

SS barracks area

Personal effects storage area ("Canada")

Disinfection building

Sewage treatment

Prisoner camps

Prisoner camps

Gas chamber and crematorium III

Route to gas chambers

Railway siding

New prisoner arrivals

Main gate

Gas chamber and crematorium II

Prisoner camps

Prisoner camps

Guard tower

North Sea

SWEDEN

Baltic Sea

DEN.

LAT.

LITH.

GER.

U.S.S.R.

Berlin

Warsaw

GERMANY

POLAND

FRANCE

CZECH.

AUST.

HUNG.

ITALY

YUGO.

ROM.

Auschwitz

N
NE
E
SE
S
SW
W
NW

Feet

0   500   1,000   2,000

Map by Gene Thorp

bodies were burned out-doors. A large pit behind Krema V served this purpose.

Auschwitz-Birkenau was built on top of a swamp, so conditions in the cramped barracks were always damp. Railroad tracks ran into the center of the camp, delivering new prisoners several times each day. Once the cars stopped at the unloading ramp, prisoners were ordered to leave their belongings behind and to line up for processing. For most of the war, women with children, as well as the elderly, were designated

Train tracks lead through the gates of the Auschwitz-Birkenau death camp in Poland.
[Mary Evans Picture Library]

The gates to Auschwitz include the phrase "Work makes you free." Before it was an extermination camp, Auschwitz was a work camp. [Mary Evans Picture Library]

for immediate extermination. After October 1944, thousands of Auschwitz prisoners were transferred to other camps as the Germans began destroying evidence of the atrocity.

In all, 80 percent of those who survived the horrible journey from their homes to Auschwitz were sent straight to the gas chambers; only those deemed capable of working as slave labor were allowed to live.

Jewish people arrive at Auschwitz. They are divided into two lines: one for the elderly, women, and children; the other for men. [Mary Evans Picture Library]

Those chosen to live were given a uniform to wear night and day—smocks for the women, pants and shirts for the men. Normal footwear was replaced by clogs made of wood or leather, but no socks, causing many prisoners to get blisters, which eventually led to infection. This frequently ended in a slow and agonizing death from gangrene.

There was no good job to have in a concentration camp. Some prisoners were chosen to serve as *kapos*—leaders of the other prisoners. Kapos got extra rations but had to live with the knowledge that they were collaborating with the Nazis by spying on their fellow prisoners, effectively ordering death sentences for those who stepped out of line.

The worst job of all went to the prisoners who looked fit and strong enough to serve as *Sonderkommandos*. They would work the ovens, obeying the SS

Women and children are liberated by Soviet troops from Auschwitz in 1945. Prisoners were required to wear thin, striped uniforms; they wore whatever other clothes they could underneath for warmth.
[Mary Evans Picture Library]

officer as he gave the order to fill the gas chambers with Zyklon B. Afterward, they had to carry dead bodies from the gas chambers to the crematoriums for burning. Each day they would grow weaker, thanks to the meager Auschwitz rations. And once they could no longer work, they themselves would be led into the gas chamber one final time.

Hundreds of barracks housed the brutalized prisoners. There were skylights but no windows. The floors were bare earth, and inmates slept on wooden bunks stacked three tiers high, covered with nothing more than rags. Rats were everywhere. The captives scratched constantly at the lice infesting their clothes and hair.

Food was precious—and hoarded. Breakfast was just a cup of imitation coffee or tea. Lunch was a cup of thin soup. And dinner was a piece of black bread and a sliver of sausage. It was common practice to take a bite of bread, then hide the rest in the lining of clothes until morning. When a prisoner died in the night, the body was quickly searched for any hidden bread.

The entire Auschwitz complex was ringed by barbed wire and overseen by armed SS guards standing in almost three dozen watchtowers. The Birkenau section backed up to a forest, and any inmate who could find a way through the wire to make a run for it was shot on sight.

Beginning in 1934, Hitler's SS was put in charge of the concentration camps that would systematically murder millions of Jews, homosexuals, Roma (gypsies), handicapped individuals, and political prisoners. The barbaric behavior of the SS was documented for all the world to see when the camps were liberated. The images from those days and the testimony of men and women who survived were used at the Nuremberg trials as evidence of the very worst of human behavior.

[below] *A barrack at Bergen-Belsen, decorated with a wall-size image of Hitler, burns after it was liberated and all the prisoners moved.* [United States Holocaust Memorial Museum, courtesy of Charles Rennie]

[next pages] *The wire perimeter fence at Auschwitz.* [Mary Evans Picture Library]

THE NUREMBERG TRIALS

O N NOVEMBER 20, 1945, IN COURTROOM 600 of the Palace of Justice in Nuremberg, Germany, the first of the Nuremberg war crimes trials began. Twenty-one of Nazi Germany's most brutal leaders sat in the dock under a bank of hot floodlights so bright that each of the prisoners had been given sunglasses. Behind them, a row of white-helmeted American military police stood at crisp attention. The eight judges—one plus an alternate from the United States, Britain, Russia, and France—took their seats at the front of the room. The proceedings started with a reading of the 24,000-word document listing the crimes for which the first group of men was being tried, including the murder of 172,000 Russians at Leningrad, the death of 780 Catholic priests at the Mauthausen concentration camp, the execution of fifty British POWs who were recaptured after their Great Escape from Stalag Luft III, the killing of soldiers in the act of surrendering, and conducting deliberate and systematic genocide, particularly against Jews, Poles, Roma, and others.

Defendants at the International Military Tribunal in Nuremberg, Germany, listen to a German translation of the proceedings through headphones. Military police guard the rear of the defendants' box. [Mary Evans Picture Library]

◆ ◆ ◆

The charges were gathered in four indictments. Many men faced more than one count:

Count One, "conspiracy to wage aggressive war," described actions committed before the war began that showed a plan to commit crimes during the war.

Count Two, "waging aggressive war" or "crimes against peace," included "the planning, preparation, initiation, and waging of wars of aggression, which were also wars in violation of international treaties, agreements, and assurances."

Count Three, "war crimes," was the more traditional violations of the laws of war, including the killing or mistreatment of prisoners of war, use of slave labor, and use of outlawed weapons.

Count Four, "crimes against humanity," involved actions related to the concentration camps, including murder, extermination, enslavement, persecution on political or racial grounds, involuntary deportation, and other inhumane acts against civilian populations.

The Nazis had kept thorough notes about their atrocities, including numbers of people arrested, numbers of people sent to the gas chambers, and experiments they performed on human beings. Those documents, as well as Nazi propaganda films and documentary films made by the Allies as the camps were liberated, were used as evidence, along with the testimony of thirty-three witnesses.

Twenty-four defendants were indicted, but one was absent (Bormann), one was deemed medically unfit, and one committed suicide before trial. In that first trial, eighteen of the twenty-four were found guilty; of these, twelve were sentenced to death. In the twelve subsequent trials at Nuremberg from 1946 to 1949, 177 political and military leaders of the Third Reich as well as German doctors, lawyers, and business leaders were tried. Twenty-four were sentenced to death by hanging, 118 were given time in prison, and thirty-five were acquitted.

LAST WILL OF ADOLF HITLER

ADOLF HITLER'S WILL AND MARRIAGE certificate were found in an envelope stored in a suitcase at the bottom of a dry well outside Munich, Germany. A Jewish American intelligence agent was shown the location after interviewing Wilhelm Zander, an aide to Martin Bormann. Zander had left Hitler's bunker on a courier mission before the Führer committed suicide, the agent discovered.

This is a translation of the will.

> *My Private Will and Testament*
> *As I did not consider that I could take responsibility, during the years of struggle, of contracting a marriage, I have now decided, before the closing of my earthly career, to take as my wife that girl who, after many years of faithful friendship, entered, of her own free will, the practically besieged town in order to share her destiny with me. At her own desire she goes as my wife with me into death. It will*

*compensate us for what we both lost through my work
in the service of my people.*

*What I possess belongs—insofar as it has any value—to
the Party. Should this no longer exist, to the State; should
the State also be destroyed, no further decision of mine is
necessary.*

*My pictures, in the collections which I have bought in
the course of years, have never been collected for private
purposes, but only for the extension of a gallery in my home
town of Linz on Donau.*

*It is my most sincere wish that this bequest may be duly
executed.*

*I nominate as my Executor my most faithful Party
comrade, Martin Bormann.*

*He is given full legal authority to make all decisions. He
is permitted to take out everything that has a sentimental
value or is necessary for the maintenance of a modest
simple life, for my brothers and sisters, also above all for the
mother of my wife and my faithful co-workers who are well
known to him, principally my old Secretaries Frau Winter,
etc. who have for many years aided me by their work.*

*I myself and my wife—in order to escape the disgrace of
deposition or capitulation—choose death. It is our wish to
be burnt immediately on the spot where I have carried out
the greatest part of my daily work in the course of twelve
years' service to my people.*

Given in Berlin, 29th April 1945, 4 a.m.
[Signed] A. Hitler
[Signed as witnesses:]
Dr. Joseph Goebbels
Martin Bormann
Colonel Nicholaus von Below

TIME LINE

April 20, 1889	Adolf Hitler is born in Braunau am Inn, Austria-Hungary, to Alios and Klara Hitler.
January 3, 1903	Hitler's father dies.
1907	Hitler moves to Vienna, Austria, to study but is rejected by both the Vienna Academy of Fine Arts and the Vienna Institute of Architecture.
1909–1913	Hitler begins to attend political meetings. He supports himself with menial jobs and by selling postcards he has illustrated.
1913	Hitler moves to Munich, Germany.
1914	World War I begins. Hitler volunteers for the German army and serves as a runner on the western front.
1919	When the war is over, Hitler joins the intelligence/propaganda section of the army. He joins the German Workers' Party, a right wing, anti-Semitic, anti-communist group.
1921	Hitler becomes the leader of the party, now called the National Socialist German Workers' Party, or the Nazi Party for short.
1923	Hitler and his party are among a group that tries to overthrow the Bavarian government. Hitler is arrested and spends nine months in jail. While there, he writes his autobiography, *Mein Kampf*.
September 1930	The Nazi Party wins 107 seats in parliament. It is now the second-largest political party in Germany.
1932	Hitler runs against Paul von Hindenburg for president of Germany. He loses but accepts the post of chancellor, second in command, in January 1933.
March 1933	The Enabling Act is passed, which gives Hitler full power. He rules that the Nazi Party is the only one allowed in the country.
August 1934	Von Hindenburg dies, and Hitler assumes the title of Führer.
1935	Hitler builds the German army and begins a draft.

March 12, 1938	The Nazi army occupies Austria, the country of Hitler's birth.
November 9–10, 1938	*Kristallnacht.* Approximately 7,500 Jewish shops and 400 synagogues are destroyed by Nazis; 20,000 people are sent to concentration camps.
1939	Germany signs a nonaggression treaty with Russia. Germany invades Poland and splits the country with Russia.
1940	The Nazis occupy Denmark, Norway, Belgium, Holland, and France.
June 22, 1941	Germany attacks Russia, despite their treaty.
December 7, 1941	The Japanese attack the U.S. naval base at Pearl Harbor, Hawaii.
February 2, 1943	Germans surrender in Stalingrad, USSR.
June 6, 1944	The Allied forces invade France on the beaches of Normandy.
July 20, 1944	Hitler survives an assassination attempt.
January 1945	Soviet troops enter Germany.
April 1945	Berlin is surrounded by Soviet troops.
April 30, 1945	Hitler and new wife Eva Braun commit suicide.
May 2, 1945	German forces in Berlin surrender.
May 7, 1945	Germany signs unconditional surrender.
May 8, 1945	V-E (Victory in Europe) Day.
August 14–15, 1945	Japanese armed forces surrender after the U.S. drops two atomic bombs.
November 20, 1945– October 1, 1946	The major war crimes trials at Nuremberg take place. Twenty-four individuals and six Nazi organizations are indicted. Twelve additional trials are held between December 9, 1946, and April 1949.

THE AUTHOR RECOMMENDS . . .

RECOMMENDED READING

Adolf Hitler and the Third Reich

Bartoletti, Susan Campbell. *Hitler Youth: Growing Up in Hitler's Shadow*. New York: Scholastic Nonfiction, 2005.

Giblin, James Cross. *The Life and Death of Adolf Hitler*. New York: Clarion, 2002.

Lace, William W. *The Nazis*. San Diego, Calif.: Lucent Books, 1998.

Marrin, Albert. *Hitler*. New York: Viking Children's Books, 1987.

Nardo, Don. *Hitler in Paris: How a Photograph Shocked a World at War*. North Mankato, Minn.: Capstone, Compass Point Books, 2014.

Samuels, Charlie. *The Third Reich, 1923–1945*. Tuson, Ariz.: Brown Bear Books, 2013.

George S. Patton

Gitlin, Martin. *George S. Patton: World War II General and Military Innovator*. Edina, Minn.: ABDO Publishing Company, 2010.

Hatch, Alden. *General George Patton: Old Blood and Guts*. New York: Sterling Publishing, 2006.

Oleksy, Walter G. *Military Leaders of World War II*. New York: Facts on File, 1994.

The Holocaust

Bachrach, Susan D. *Tell Them We Remember*: *The Story of the Holocaust*. Boston: Little, Brown & Company, 1994.

Fishkin, Rebecca Love. *Heroes of the Holocaust*. Mankato, Minn.: Capstone, Compass Point Books, 2011.

Lee, Carol Ann. *Anne Frank and the Children of the Holocaust*. New York: Viking, 2006.

Wood, Angela Gluck. *Holocaust: The Events and Their Impact on Real People*. New York: DK Publishing, 2007.

World War II

Adams, Simon. *Eyewitness: World War II*. New York: DK Publishing, 2014.

Ambrose, Stephen E. *The Good Fight: How World War II Was Won*. New York: Atheneum Books for Young Readers, 2001.

Nicholson, Dorinda Makanaōnalani. *Remember World War II: Kids Who Survived Tell Their Stories*. Washington, D.C.: National Geographic, 2005.

Raum, Elizabeth. *A World War II Timeline*. North Mankato, Minn.: Capstone Press, 2014.

RECOMMENDED VIEWING

Dear Uncle Adolf: The Germans and Their Führer. Michael Kloft, director. DVD. First Run Features, 2011. 60 minutes, NR.

The Nazis: A Warning from History. Laurence Rees, writer and producer. DVD. BBC Video, 2005. 300 minutes, NR.

The World at War. DVD. A&E Home Video, 2004. 1,357 minutes, NR.

BIBLIOGRAPHY

Barron, Leo. *Patton at the Battle of the Bulge: How the General's Tanks Turned the Tide at Bastogne*. New York: Penguin, NAL Caliber, 2014.

Blumenson, Martin. *The Patton Papers*. Vol. 2, *1940–1945*. Boston: Houghton Mifflin, 1974.

Brighton, Terry. *Patton, Montgomery, Rommel: Masters of War*. New York: Crown Publishers, 2008.

Fest, Joachim. *Inside Hitler's Bunker: The Last Days of the Third Reich*. Translated by Margot Bettauer Dembo. New York: Farrar, Straus and Giroux, 2002.

Freytag von Loringhoven, Bernd, and François D'Alançon. *In the Bunker with Hitler*. New York: Pegasus Books, 2005.

Giblin, James Cross. *The Life and Death of Adolf Hitler*. New York: Clarion, 2002.

Hirshson, Stanley P. *General Patton: A Soldier's Life*. New York: HarperCollins Publishers, 2002.

Kershaw, Ian. *Hitler, 1936–1945: Nemesis*. New York: W.W. Norton and Company, 2000.

O'Reilly, Bill and Martin Dugard. *Killing Patton*. New York: Henry Holt and Co., 2014.

Patton, George S. *War As I Knew It*. Boston: Houghton Mifflin, 1947.

Showalter, Dennis. *Patton and Rommel: Men of War in the Twentieth Century*. New York: Berkley Publishing Group, 2005.

Stone, David. *Hitler's Army: The Men, Machines, and Organization, 1939–1945*. Minneapolis, Minn.: MBI Publishing, Zenith Press, 2009.

SOURCES

TRAVELED TO MANY OF THE sites mentioned in this book and spoke to people who remembered the last months of World War II in Europe. My research also took me to various archives, museums, and the official U.S. Army histories. In particular, the presidential libraries of Franklin Roosevelt and Harry Truman, and the National Archives were of great assistance.

The Topography of Terror site in Berlin offered a chilling look at Nazi Germany. It is built atop the former site of Gestapo headquarters, next to a small remaining section of the Berlin Wall.

The General Patton Memorial Museum at Chiriaco Summit in California's Mojave Desert contains a vast and diverse amount of Patton memorabilia, including several tanks displayed in the desert surrounding the museum.

The town of Bastogne pays homage to its American defenders and the Battle of the Bulge each year in December. The 101st Airborne's former barracks and the site of General McAuliffe's headquarters are an operational Belgian military facility now, but visitors can take a guided tour of the Bastogne Barracks interpretation center, featuring a recreation of General McAuliffe's basement office.

World War II has been written about extensively, but Cornelius Ryan's *The Last Battle* and Rick Atkinson's *The Guns at Last Light* are loaded with detail and action. *The Victors*, by Stephen E. Ambrose, takes the reader onto the battlefield through the eyes of ordinary soldiers, and in vivid fashion. For a look at the war from a command point of view, Omar Bradley's *A Soldier's Story* is self-effacing and an easy read. While there are too many books detailing the war to list in this space, some that were very helpful in providing background nuance include *Darkness Visible: Memoir of a World War II Combat Photographer*, by Charles Eugene Sumners; *World War II in Numbers*, by Peter Doyle; *Patton,*

Montgomery, Rommel: Masters of War, by Terry Brighton; *The Nuremberg Trials: The Nazis and Their Crimes Against Humanity,* by Paul Roland; and *The Battle for Western Europe, Fall 1944: An Operational Assessment,* by John A. Adams.

The Battle of the Bulge, milestone of the war, has been covered at great length, but the books we relied on were Robert E. Merriam's *The Battle of the Bulge; Troy H. Middleton: A Biography,* by Frank James Price; *Battle: The Story of the Bulge,* by John Toland; *11 Days in December: Christmas at the Bulge, 1944,* by Stanley Weintraub; *Alamo in the Ardennes,* by John C. McManus; *Against the Panzers: United States Infantry Versus German Tanks, 1944–1945,* by Allyn R. Vannoy and Jay Karamales; *The Ardennes on Fire: The First Day of the German Assault,* by Timothy J. Thompson; *Fatal Crossroads: The Untold Story of the Malmédy Massacre at the Battle of the Bulge,* by Danny S. Parker; *The Ghost in General Patton's Third Army: The Memoirs of Eugene G. Schulz During His Service in the United States Army in World War II,* by Eugene G. Schulz; *Battle of the Bulge 1944 (2): Bastogne,* by Steven J. Zaloga; and the underrated *Once Upon a Time in War: The 99th Division in World War II,* by Robert E. Humphrey.

To step inside Adolf Hitler's world is frightening, to say the least. It helped to follow the research of other writers who had gone there already, including firsthand accounts by Otto Skorzeny (*Skorzeny's Special Missions: The Memoirs of Hitler's Most Daring Commando*) and Traudl Junge (*Hitler's Last Secretary: A Firsthand Account of Life with Hitler*). In addition, *Inside Hitler's Bunker: The Last Days of the Third Reich,* by Joachim Fest; *Hitler,* by Joachim Fest; *Hitler: An Illustrated Life,* by Robin Cross; and *Hitler: A Biography,* by Ian Kershaw were all spectacular.

A great amount of archival detail is available about the big three Allied leaders. Books of note were *The Lesser Terror: Soviet State Security, 1939–1953,* by Michael Parrish; *Joseph Stalin: A Biographical Companion,* by Helen

Rappaport; *My Dear Mr. Stalin: The Complete Correspondence of Franklin D. Roosevelt and Joseph V. Stalin*, edited by Susan Butler; *No Ordinary Time: Franklin and Eleanor Roosevelt: The Home Front in World War II*, by Doris Kearns Goodwin; *Defending the West: The Truman-Churchill Correspondence, 1945–1960*, edited by G.W. Sand; *The Last Thousand Days of the British Empire*, by Peter Clarke; and *The Road to Berlin*, volume two of *Stalin's War with Germany*, by John Erickson.

Thanks to these authors, and to those whose books are not mentioned but whose research aided in building this narrative.

INDEX

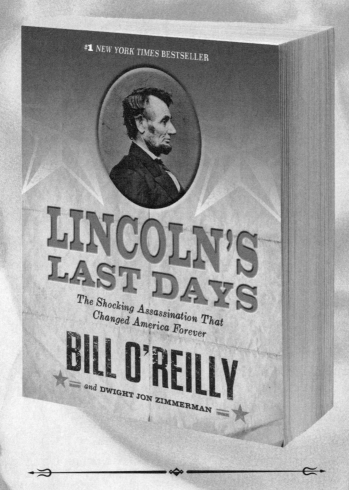

THE SHOCKING ASSASSINATION
that changed America forever...

LINCOLN'S LAST DAYS

is history like you've never read before.
Turn the page for a sneak peek.

SATURDAY, MARCH 4, 1865
Washington, D.C.

A BRAHAM LINCOLN, the man with six weeks to live, is anxious. The speech he is about to give is vital to the peace of the country. Since the Battle of Fort Sumter took place in South Carolina in April 1861, the United States has been a "house divided," locked in a civil war between the free North and the slaveholding South. Led by South Carolina, a total of eleven slaveholding states in the South have left the Union and formed a separate nation, the Confederate States of America. The states that seceded felt that maintaining the institution of slavery was essential to their economy and they were willing to leave the Union rather than outlaw slavery.

Lincoln tried to stop the states from leaving, but they refused his peaceful appeals. When Confederate troops fired on Union troops at Fort Sumter, Lincoln had no choice but to go to war. This civil war has not only divided the nation, it has also split countless families, pitting fathers against sons, and brothers against brothers. It is

Abraham Lincoln delivering his second inaugural address, March 4, 1865.
John Wilkes Booth is in the crowd to the right and above where the president stands.

a situation that even affects Lincoln's family. His wife, Mary Todd Lincoln, has relatives fighting for the Confederacy. Much blood—too much blood—has been shed in this terrible conflict. Lincoln sighs, hoping that it will end soon, and with the Union victorious.

Fifty thousand men and women are standing in pouring rain and ankle-deep mud to watch Abraham Lincoln take the oath of office to begin his second term.

Lincoln steps up to the podium and delivers an eloquent appeal for reunification in his second inaugural address.

"With malice toward none, with charity for all, with firmness in the right as God gives us to see the right, let us strive on to finish the work we are in, to bind up the nation's wounds, to care for him who shall have borne the battle and for his widow and his orphan, to do all which may achieve and cherish a just and lasting peace among ourselves and with all nations," the president says humbly. As he speaks, the sun bursts through the clouds, its light surrounding the tall and outwardly serene Lincoln.

Although Lincoln does not know this, 120 miles south of Washington, at the important railroad and communications center of Petersburg, Virginia, a siege that started in June 1864 is nearing its end. The Confederate Army of Northern Virginia, under the command of General Robert E. Lee, has been pinned in and around the city for more than 250 days by Union forces under the command of General Ulysses S. Grant. Lee knew if he didn't defend Petersburg, the road to the Confederate capital of Richmond would be wide open. The capture of Richmond by Union troops would be a powerful symbolic victory, telling everyone that the end of the Confederacy was near. So Lee ordered his army to stay, dig trenches, and fight.

But now, in April 1865, Lee's army is weak. At this point, if Lee remains and continues to defend Petersburg, his forces will be destroyed by Grant's Army of the Potomac, which grows stronger in men and guns with each passing week. Lee knows that Grant is preparing for an overwhelming attack. Lee plans to have his army slip out of Petersburg and escape south to the Carolinas before that happens. If he succeeds, Lincoln's prayer for a reunified United States of America may never be answered. America will continue to be divided into a North and a South, a United States of America and a Confederate States of America.

⬥ ⬥✳⬥ ⬥

Lincoln's inaugural speech is a performance worthy of a great dramatic actor. And indeed, one of America's most famous actors stands just yards away as the president speaks. Twenty-six-year-old John Wilkes Booth is inspired by the president's words—though not in the way Lincoln intends.

The president has ambitious plans for his second term in office. Ending the war and healing the war-torn nation are Lincoln's overriding ambitions. He will use every last bit of his trademark determination to see these goals realized; nothing must stand in his way.

But evil knows no boundaries. And a most powerful evil—in the person of John Wilkes Booth and his fellow conspirators—is now focused on Abraham Lincoln.

John Wilkes Booth.

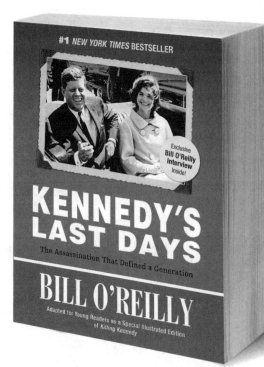

IT WAS

THE MOST NOTORIOUS CRIME
OF THE TWENTIETH CENTURY. . . .

#1 *NEW YORK TIMES* BESTSELLER

Exclusive
**Bill O'Reilly
Interview**
Inside!

KENNEDY'S
LAST DAYS
The Assassination That Defined a Generation

BILL O'REILLY
Adapted for Young Readers as a Special Illustrated Edition
of *Killing Kennedy*

KENNEDY'S LAST DAYS
is history like you've never read before.

*Kennedy places his hand on an 1850 edition of the Bible brought
from Ireland by his ancestors.* [JFK Presidential Library and Museum]

CHAPTER ONE

JANUARY 20, 1961

Washington, D.C. 12:51 P.M.

THE MAN WITH FEWER THAN THREE YEARS to live places his left hand on the Bible.

Earl Warren, chief justice of the United States Supreme Court, stands before him reciting the Presidential Oath of Office. "You, John Fitzgerald Kennedy, do solemnly swear . . ."

"I, John Fitzgerald Kennedy, do solemnly swear," the new president repeats in his Boston accent.

John Kennedy was born into wealth and has a refined manner of speaking that would seem to distance him from many people. But he is an enthusiastic and easily likable man. He won the popular vote over Richard Nixon by a razor-thin margin, getting just 49 percent of the total votes. So not everyone loves JFK, but this is an exciting moment for the country.

". . . that you will faithfully execute the office of president of the United States . . ."

"... that I will faithfully execute the office of president of the United States. ..."

Eighty million Americans are watching the inauguration on television. Twenty thousand more are there in person. Eight inches of thick, wet snow have fallen on Washington, D.C., overnight. Spectators wrap their bodies in sleeping bags, blankets, thick sweaters, and winter coats—anything to stay warm.

The Marine Band stands in front of the Capitol during the inauguration ceremonies. [JFK Presidential Library and Museum]

But John Kennedy ignores the cold. He has even removed his overcoat. At age 43, JFK exudes fearlessness and vigor. His lack of coat, top hat, scarf, or gloves is intentional—this helps to confirm his athletic image. He is trim and just a shade over six feet tall, with greenish-gray eyes, a dazzling smile, and a deep tan, thanks to a recent vacation in Florida.

". . . and will to the best of your ability . . ."

". . . and will to the best of my ability . . ."

In the sea of dignitaries and friends all around him, there are three people vital to Kennedy. The first is his younger brother Bobby, soon to be appointed U.S. attorney general. The president values him for his honesty and knows that Bobby will always tell him the truth, no matter how brutal it may be.

Behind the president is the new vice president, Lyndon Baines Johnson, who is often called LBJ. It can be said, and Johnson himself believes, that Kennedy won the presidency because Johnson was on the ticket, which allowed them to win the most votes in Johnson's home state of Texas.

Finally, the new president glances toward his young wife, standing behind Justice Warren. Jackie's eyes sparkle. Despite her happy face today, Jackie Kennedy has already known tragedy during their seven years of marriage. She miscarried their first child, and the second was a stillborn baby girl. But she has also enjoyed the birth of two healthy children, Caroline and John Jr., and the stunning rise of her dashing young husband from a Massachusetts politician to president of the United States.

*John F. Kennedy takes the oath of office, administered
by Chief Justice Earl Warren.* [© Bettmann/Corbis]

". . . preserve, protect, and defend the Constitution of the United States."

". . . preserve, protect, and defend the Constitution of the United States."

Kennedy's predecessor, Dwight Eisenhower, stands near Jackie. Behind Kennedy stand Richard Nixon, Eisenhower's vice president and Kennedy's adversary in the presidential campaign, and Harry Truman, the Democratic president who held office before Eisenhower.

Normally, having just one of these dignitaries at an event means heightened security. Having all of them at the inaugural, sitting together, is a security nightmare.

The Secret Service is on high alert. Its job is to protect the president. The leader of the service, Chief U. E. Baughman, has been in charge since Truman was president. His agents scan the crowd, nervous about the proximity of the huge audience. One well-trained fanatic with a pistol could kill the new president, two former presidents, and a pair of vice presidents with five crisp shots.

". . . So help you, God."

". . . So help me, God."

The oath complete, Kennedy shakes Chief Justice Warren's hand, then those of Johnson and Nixon and finally Eisenhower.

Kennedy is the youngest president ever elected. Eisenhower is one of the oldest. The great divide in their ages also represents two very different generations of Americans—and two very different views of America. Those watching in person and those watching on TV agree: The future looks limitless and bright.

LES NOUVELLES DU MATIN

Directeur: JEAN MARIN

La victoire en chantant

Prix : 1 f

MARDI 8 MAI 1945

EN EUROPE, DEPUIS CETTE NUIT A 23 h. 1

LA GUERRE EST FINIE

La capitulation sans conditions de l'Allema

sera annoncée officiellem

LONDRES, 7 mai. — La B.B.C. a
von Krosigk, a déclaré à la radio de Flensb
lemand avait accepté ce jour la reddition in
La capitulation prend effet dans la

MERCI
par JEAN MARIN

C'est à lui que je pense d'abord en cette nuit d'une
.... enfin, la guerre agonise ....

A REIMS, DAN

REIMS, 7 mai. — On annonce of
La reddition a été signée cette nu
..........hower. Le colo

Frankfurte

HERAUSGEBER: DIE AMERIKANISCHE 12. HEERESGRUPPE

Bedingungslose Kap

Am 8. Mai 1945 en
Urkunden von K

Die Sieger sprechen

am Nachmittag des 8. Mai, der von den
Alliierten offiziell als Siegertag bezeichnet
wird, prüfen würde, hielten die führenden
Staatsmänner der Alliierten wichtige Staats-

Truman: Sieg der Freiheit

Der Präsident der Vereinigten Staaten er-

EDITION
de la
VICTOIRE

V I